Remember When...

How to unlock your life story

by JOHN HOCKNEY

citrus press

Dedicated to my wife Helen,
whose love and support for this project
has helped make it a reality.

My sincerest thanks and appreciation to those who have encouraged and helped: Sue Alvarez and Christine Greenough for their companionship, ideas and sheer fun as we developed reminiscing programmes; Anne and David Bottomley for their kindness and hospitality when researching information in Bradford; Trish Daly for her help with the Irish perspective; Souad Daizli for her help with the Lebanese story; Lucia D'Allessandro for her help with the Italian background; Paul and Jean Hockney for their memories of earlier family days; Philip and Mary Hockney for their generous and timely gift of a laptop computer; Margaret Hockney for her total belief and encouragement in my concept; David Hockney for teaching me "looking and awareness"; my storyteller colleague, Donna Jacobsife, for her Jewish stories; Nabil and Greta Marzouk for *Sweethearts, Courting and Getting Wed*; Hai Loc Nguyen for his Vietnamese story; Bill Petinos for his help with the Greek perspective; Atchara Pradit in Thailand; Mary, Ruth, Jim, Carmel and Helen Rafferty; Catharine Retter, my publisher, for her faith, help and suggestions.

Contents

Introduction

Have you ever gone into a room to do something and forgotten why you were there?

So have I!

It seems to happen more frequently as we get older, but luckily it doesn't usually stop us recalling distant memories. They can bring us back to happy and joyous times or act as a familiar companion in our solitary hours. Even sad memories can help us remember that good times eventually followed.

Memories, when shared with our grandchildren, can bring looks of disbelief at a world that doesn't exist for them. Haven't you sometimes wished your children and their children could know what it was like back then; what sort of family they came from; how different life was before fast food, fast transport and fast emails. Perhaps people might at last understand why you don't like war movies, why you always felt the value of a good education, or why you get sentimental over Labradors.

How many of us have wished our own parents or grandparents had written down their stories before it was too late? Perhaps you've also thought of recording your life story—but where and how to begin? How can you possibly remember it all? Do you have to start at the beginning? Do you have to include everything, or is it all right to leave some things out? Don't you have to have creative writing skills?

This book will help you look at your personal memories and access those stories you select to pass on to your children, grandchildren or friends. It has trigger questions to help you recall and organise your thoughts. They're questions that have been formed from my experiences as a professional storyteller in sessions with seniors, community groups, festivals, schools, retirement villages and nursing homes—as well as advice from diversional therapists, nursing sisters and professional colleagues. (For more information on how this book came to be, see A Note from the Author, page 104.)

They're questions that can also be used by people of all ages as a tool to explore their family backgrounds, or can act as an invaluable reference for schools, diversional therapists and those working in aged care.

How to Begin

- Select a subject that interests you from the list of contents and go to that chapter.
- Read the introductory story example.
- Follow up with the *Unlocking Memories* questions and scribble down a list of any thoughts that come to you, and you are on your way.
- Use power words to discover more memories. For example, expand the story (and your memories) by asking yourself:

What happened? What was the subject or event all about?
How did it happen? What were the circumstances that lead to this event?
When did it happen? The date and period of life (young/adult etc.).
Why did it happen? What were the reasons behind the event?
Where did it happen? Describe the place and environment.
Who did it happen to? Who were the people attending the event.

- Add your own additional unlocked memories as they come to you.
- Research any additional information to enhance your story if you wish. (See chapter on Researching your story.)
- Look at old photographs, newspapers and magazines of the same period you remember.

Everyone has a story to tell and everyone's story is different depending on family background, attitudes, personal life experiences, cultural background, levels of prosperity and individual interests. Some stories may be humorous and fun, others may describe courage over adversity, or pride through accomplishment or struggle. *Remember When* has been structured to let you think about and record a certain time or subject that is important to you without necessarily having to start at the very beginning.

No, you don't need great writing skills. Very often it's the simple everyday happenings of the past that create the most fascinating stories.

You don't need to feel daunted by the challenge of writing a whole life story. The book's structure lets you dip into subjects one at a time, at your own pace, in whichever order you choose and wherever your memories take you. At the beginning of each chapter is a short story to show you how simple it can be.

Your memories and words are drawn from your own perspective, how you saw life at a particular time. It will differ from how your parents, brothers or sisters saw or experienced it.

Writing Tip

Once you have collated your memories, you can help bring them alive by adding your recollections of *emotions* you felt at the time; the *smell* of a room or outdoors; the *taste* of food or drink; the sense of *touch* of the clothes you wore or what you were sitting or standing on; the *sound* of someone's voice or music/machinery/gunfire/birds you heard at the time. They will help personalise the description of your story.

From my childhood I distinctly remember the smell of the countryside in summer, a sweet perfume mixed with new mown hay, flowers and shrubs. I can still recall the thrill of feeling the wind rushing through my hair and brushing against my cheeks as I rode my bicycle down a steep hill.

Don't forget that an important part of any story is also the teller: you. It's about your relationship to the stories, events and people you write about. Without this, it becomes just a record of the facts.

The story will begin to unlock your "voice", allowing the listener or reader to feel your emotions and recollections and enjoy the wisdom, laughter or frailty of the particular story you share with them.

Birthdays

Jelly wobbles, the key-to-the-door,
name days and pass-the-parcel.

How did you celebrate your childhood birthdays?

Birthdays were always an exciting celebration in our family. As the youngest, I longed to be as old as my brothers and sister. They always seemed to have a better time than I did.

Who came to your parties: friends, relatives?

I celebrated birthdays with an entourage of aunts, uncles, cousins and "adopted aunts" who joined family and friends to wish a happy birthday.

What did you eat?

There was always a simple cake with some icing and candles, games of musical chairs, pass-the-parcel, postman's knock, and often a singsong. Party food was invariably jam and bread, and perhaps wobbly jelly or blancmange.

My friend, Trish Daly from Ireland, remembers that meringues were a feature at every birthday party for her. They were specially made by her mother, and the secret ingredient was that they were finished off in the clothes drying cabinet to make the meringues rise!

Were you ever taken on a special outing on your birthday? Where to? With whom?

I remember once being taken to see Walt Disney's Bambi by an infant teacher, and having an ice cream, a real treat. It was the first time I had ever been to a cinema.

What was the best present you ever received? Who gave you the present?

One of the best presents I ever received was a Biro pen. It was quite revolutionary at that time. It didn't need ink, just a replacement refill. My schoolteacher considered it a modern invention, unworthy of the esteemed nibbed pen and confiscated it until home time. Soon after my birthday, I was playing in a field and lost my treasured pen. A year later, while playing in the same field—now full of cabbages—there it was, and it still wrote beautifully.

When you reached twenty-one, did you have a special party? Where was it? Who came?

Paul, my eldest brother, was the first to reach twenty-one and was given a special twenty-first birthday party. I was thirteen at the time and was wide-mouthed and goggle-eyed at all his presents. I had never seen so many.

There was a special twenty-first-birthday cake, and relatives and friends all helped to make salmon paste and potted meat sandwiches, cakes and hot tea. I think there was jelly and trifle pudding too.

Were birthday celebrations influenced by different cultural backgrounds in your family?

My publisher, Catharine, shares a charming birthday tale from her Dutch origins. She recalls that her mother always draped the birthday person's chair in the dining room with the national flag and a big orange velvet sash, and arranged flowers into the sash at the back of the chair. She remembers how very special this made her feel on her birthday, and wishes the custom was still observed.

Perhaps you came from a background where name days were celebrated more so than birthdays?

In Greece, children are named after saints, and naming ceremonies are followed by happy family gatherings with lots of food, laughter and dancing. I am fortunate to have Greek friends, Bill and Penny Petinos, and when I am invited to join their family and friends I know it is going to be a memorable occasion. Their hospitality is always warm and welcoming. "That's normal", says Bill, "because, Greeks love a party."

Bill was actually named "Vassil", which is "Basil" in Greek and relates to St Basil, a saint similar to St Nicholas or Father Christmas. (Now I know why Bill is always so giving.)

When his parents arrived in Australia, Bill was only one-and-a-half, and when they passed through Customs the officers asked his name.

"Vassil", his parents told them.

"Vassil? Vassil? Don't know any Vassil, let's just call him Billy", they said. So Vassil became Billy in Australia, and he has been known as Billy or Bill ever since.

Perhaps you may recall a family, or local custom or tradition that you can include in your story?

Unlocking more birthday memories

What is the first birthday party you can remember?

What makes it stick in your memory?

What do you remember about reaching "double figures" or becoming a teenager?

Have you kept any birthday cards from your childhood?

Did you have a special party dress or suit for your birthday clothes?

What colour and style?

Which birthday was the best you ever remember? Why?

What games did you play at your birthday party?

Did you ever make presents or only buy them? What did you make?

Were you given the key of the door when you reached twenty-one?

Did your mother ever decorate your birthday cake in a special way?

What was the most exciting birthday present you ever received?

Did you ever eat too much at your own birthday party? What happened?

Was there a time you never celebrated a birthday? Why?

Can you remember any of the childhood friends who came to your birthday parties, or whose birthday parties you went to?

Do you still keep in touch on birthdays?

Childhood

Basin cuts, Robin Hood and penfriends.

What is your date of birth? What time were you born? In which city and country were you born? Were you born in hospital or at home?

I was eight months in the womb when War was declared in September 1939. The British Government evacuated my mother, brothers and sister just a few miles over the Lancashire border. It was the first time the family had been separated and the circumstances made it very stressful for my mother.

My brothers and sister were billeted with unknown families in Nelson while my mother was sent to Langroyd Hall, a large ancestral house that had been converted into a makeshift maternity hospital in Colne. There were no friendly faces to help or comfort her, and beds were just mattresses laid on the floor. On October 23, at 5.45 am, I arrived into the big wide world. Almost immediately I contracted eczema, a nervous rash… I wonder why?

What is your earliest childhood memory?

My earliest childhood memory is quite vivid. I was lying in a pram being pushed down a street. The pram hood was up, and I was tucked in with a cover over me. It was dark, and I remember gaslights approach and fade away overhead, casting intermittent light into the pram's interior. I distinctly remember the wheels of the pram thudding over the flagged paving. My father repaired prams and I may already have been three or four years old. Perhaps he had taken me along while he picked up a repair or renovation as it was easier to push me in the pram than have me running next to him trying to keep up.

Everything seemed bigger when I was a child: people, buildings, trees, and buses. I found the high barber's chair quite threatening when I had to go for my first haircut. The barber had a wooden insert with a cushion for children to kneel on, so when I sat on it my head was at the appropriate cutting level. When the barber first used electric clippers to trim my hair, I peed on his cushion. He was not amused, but neither was I. Haircuts in those days were referred to as basin cuts, being short back and sides with a parting, and plastered down with cream or dressing that made your hair so stiff not a hair escaped its grip.

What games did you play: skipping, whip and top, hopscotch, hide and seek, rounders and follow the leader? Who did you play with? Where did you play: garden, street, park, fields?

I grew up in Eccleshill village, about two miles from Bradford. The village straddled the top of the Pennine Mountains with views extending towards Leeds through the Airedale valley. The green fields and small woods provided great adventures for little boys, and at a railway goods yard nearby we would lean over the wooden fence and look into the workplace for German prisoners of war who were easily identified by their navy blue jackets and a large yellow circle on their backs. They seemed, to us, to be ordinary men, and offered friendly words back to us in broken English. It was inconceivable to us that they could kill people.

Did you have a craft or pastime? What was it? Do you still have anything you made?

Margaret, my sister, taught me "French knitting", using a cotton reel with small nails in the top. The knitting fed through the hole in the empty cotton reel and came out at the bottom. Different coloured wools could be added at any time and, when sewn together, made colourful mats for vases or on a dressing table. Sometimes, as presents, we made lavender bags, using muslin with a bit of lavender. They were to be put into drawers or cupboards to provide a fragrance.

What imaginary games did you play?

Imagination was the key to my childhood games and dreams. I could be anybody, and be in any far off country I chose. There were plenty of trees to climb,

5

and villains to fight. I became Sir Lancelot or Robin Hood, a stick became an imaginary sword, and a dustbin lid a shield. We were never allowed toy guns, but two fingers with the thumb over the middle and first finger was just as good.

I never remember being bored, there was always so much to do. Even a simple hoop became a steering wheel for a bus. I had a driver's white coat with a red collar, my lips made the noise of the engine as I changed gear and stopped at lampposts pretending they were bus stops. To me I was really driving a bus.

During the winter months snow sledging was our main thrill, speeding down the hills on perfectly white virgin snow with the cold wind cutting into faces. The cold never seemed to matter even though I went home with knees chapped from the icy winds and snow, and legs welted from wellington boots that had rubbed on the bare skin exposed below my short trousers.

Did you have a penfriend? Do you still keep in contact? Where did they live? Have you kept any letters? What did you write about?

To encourage letter writing, and to learn about life in different countries and cultures we were encouraged to have penfriends. My brother, David, had a penfriend in America who sent him boxes of bubble gum, which I thought tasted like Germolene, (an antiseptic ointment). I wrote to a boy in Calais, and to Billy Fordham who lived in a National Children's home in Cheshire. We never met our penfriends, but I remember the thrill of the postman delivering a letter with my name on it!

Unlocking more childhood memories

Do you have a copy of your birth certificate?

Does the birth certificate mention the occupations of your father and mother? What were they?

Were you baptised or christened into a religion?

Are you aware of any other special events that happened on your birth date or during the month or year you were born?

What star sign are you?

Did you have a favourite or special toy? What was it?

Which organization of Scouts/Guides/Cubs/Brownies/Boys Brigade did you belong? What proficiency badges did you get?

Did you go camping? What was it like? How did you light a fire and cook?

Who was your best friend when growing up? Are you still best friends?

Did you listen to children's radio programmes? What were they? Which was your favourite?

Which children's books or comics did you read?

Were you ever naughty (smoking, alcohol, sex)?

Were you caught or found out?

What punishment did you get?

Did you have a pet? What was it?

Were you alone responsible for looking after it, or was it shared with other family members?

How did you look after it?

Can you recall the happiest event of your childhood? What was it?

Can you recall the saddest or most hurtful event of your childhood? What was it?

Christmas and Chanukah

Snow, pulling Santa's beard and sunburn.

In England, Christmas meant that winter was well and truly entrenched. It meant the hustle and bustle of shopping, cooking and baking, with secretive bundles hidden in wardrobes and under beds.

I willingly accompanied my mother into town to help carry groceries and goodies just so that I could see the street decorations with their twinkling lights, and shop windows bursting with ideas for presents.

When did you find out the truth about Santa? How did it happen? Did it spoil Christmas for you?

I could never understand why there was a Santa Claus near the bus stop in Forster Square, then another at the bottom of the market steps, and still another at the top end of the market. Mum assured me they were pretend Santas, helping the real one who couldn't be everywhere. I totally accepted her reasoning but thought it strange Santa would not give me a present unless I gave him threepence. I found out some years later they were pedlars trying to make a quick quid before Christmas.

Was your house decorated for Christmas?

We had only homemade Christmas decorations. Paper chains and lanterns were the most popular and easy to make. They were strung across the living and front rooms and tied from each corner of the room to the centre light fitting, then decorated with a sprig of holly and mistletoe. Simple and crude though they must have been, to us they looked bright and gay, and we'd made them!

My wife's family in Australia could not afford real Christmas trees when she was little so Dad Rafferty would cut a large branch from a tree in the garden and the girls made decorations from the *Women's Weekly*, cutting carefully around any smiling face they could find and suspending it from the branches. When it was freshly cut, the tree was bright and the decorations cheerful, but it was never long before the branches wilted in the Christmas heat, and the paper with the smiling faces began to droop.

How did you spend Christmas as a child?

Lucia d'Alessandro remembers growing up in the north of Italy and spending Christmas at her grandmother's, only a short walk from home. Christmas Eve was the important time for Italian families, and a large pine tree was decorated with oranges, mandarins, nougat and sweets ready to be removed by tiny fingers at the first available opportunity.

How important was the religious part of Christmas to your family?

At midnight, the family attended Christmas mass and Lucia still remembers her awe at the lighted candles that reflected on the upturned faces of children, the beautiful Christmas music that filled the church, and the excitement of gazing up at the manger and crib.

How different this is to my wife's memories. Dad Rafferty took the family to church at Christmas, instructing them to sit when he sat, stand when he stood, kneel when he knelt, and pray when he prayed. No one was to speak and all had to pay attention to what the priest was saying and woe-betide anyone caught with their eyes admiringly transfixed on her new black shoes worn for the first time that day.

What sort of food did you eat on Christmas Day or on Chanukah? Do you remember cooking smells? Can you describe them?

A few months before Christmas, my mother started making Christmas puddings and mince for mince pies. Everything had to be made, no packet products, even the suet had to be grated from a block. The mince pie mixture had to be stirred continuously (and quickly tasted when Mum wasn't looking). The pudding mix always got a lot of helpers so we all got a turn at cleaning the bowl and licking the uncooked mixture off our fingers.

I often went shopping with Mum, and walking through the meat market, I always looked in awe at the displays of dead pheasants and rabbits, chickens, ducks and geese that were nearly the same size as me. With laden bags, we made our way to the bus stop, and if Mum was in the mood I'd be treated to a plate of mushy peas with mint sauce and a glass of hot raspberry drink to keep out the cold and warm my toes.

When my wife was growing up, her mother kept hens and roosters, and each year a hen was selected for the Christmas feast. Christmas dinner was *Christmas dinner* in the Rafferty household. It was always the same, wherever they lived and whether it was 18 $^{\circ}$C or 40 $^{\circ}$C. Dad Rafferty wasn't well-skilled in chook killing, and every year the children gathered round to watch, and inevitably when Dad Rafferty lopped off the chook's head its body kept running round the yard. Each year the children screamed and quickly ran to hide from the sight.

Mum Rafferty took over, removed the innards and filled the cavity with homemade stuffing, and placed the chook into the wood-fired stove lit with old railway sleeper kindling. With the chicken feast came roast potatoes, pumpkin, or sweet potato and peas with lashings of homemade gravy.

Was the festive season a time for family or a time for inviting someone less fortunate or lonely? How did it feel? Where did you spend the day: at home, with relatives or friends?

There was always company in our house on Christmas Day, whether relatives or some person Mum thought would have otherwise been alone. They were happy times: a cosy fire, a lot of laughter and a great deal of love emanated from 18 Hutton Terrace in Bradford.

My wife's family also had a regular Christmas Day guest. It was the only time of year he would visit but, even so, the Rafferty children did not warmly welcome him into their midst. Their Christmas visitor was meticulous about correctly digesting his food and carefully chewed every mouthful. The Rafferty children were used to eating quickly, and waited impatiently for their guest to finish. Being careful not to get caught—by their parents or their guest—the children imitated his careful chewing, perhaps hoping to help him along and speed up the process.

After dinner, the Rafferty girls were relegated the task of washing up the enormous collection of pots, pans and dishes and the kitchen soon resounded with their harmonic voices singing "R-A–double F- E- R-T-Y spells Rafferty", and a Christmas Day passed for another year.

Did you grow up in a country with cold or hot Christmases? Which do you prefer hot or cold?

I still find it hard to relate to Christmas in Australia, even though I have lived here twice as long as in England. It is so hot in December, and doesn't seem to fit the tradition of Christmas.

I vividly remember my first Australian Christmas. I had been invited by some newfound friends to spend the day with them at Bondi Beach. As I was not looking forward to eating a hot Christmas dinner indoors on a hot day, I willingly accepted.

The temperature soared to over 95 °F. I had a wonderful time splashing in the surf, watching the bright blue waves pound the beach and the surfboard riders eager to catch the next perfect wave. I was enjoying my friends, the beach and the ocean, oblivious to time, and forgetting all about the festive season. I was also oblivious to the strong sun on my white body until, a few hours later, when I felt a hot tightness on my back, arms, legs and face. I woke up in the emergency section of Prince of Wales Hospital being treated for third degree sunburn. I could not move for days and the pain was excruciating. Blisters the size of golf balls bubbled on my skin, and the only thing like Christmas was my colour: red!

Remember When…

Were you happy with your presents or were you jealous of what others received?

Child jealousies sometimes crept up at Christmas time. The Rafferty sisters, Catherine and Carmel, shared a room and, one Christmas, a brightly painted scooter left by Santa stood at the foot of Carmel's bed, but strangely, by morning had moved itself to the foot of Catherine's bed. The din, which erupted in the girl's bedroom upon discovery, drowned the strains of *Peace on earth and mercy mild* from the radio.

Have you ever helped at a charity lunch on Christmas Day? Where was it? Did you enjoy it?

Ted Noffs from the Wayside Chapel created the closest feelings to the Christmases of my childhood. He offered free lunches and entertainment for the poor and lonely and I was pleased to help on many occasions. At those times it felt like the true spirit of Christmas.

The festive season is an important time for many religions. Perhaps your family celebrates Chanukah? What does it mean to you?

A Jewish friend of mine in Los Angeles told me this story about her grandfather in Poland. For him, Chanukah brings back memories of when he was ten. It happens every year: the same memory, and the same thanksgiving.

Every Chanukah he stands with his wife, Esther, and children Hila, Michael and Simon beside him. His hand strikes the match to bring the wick of the *Shamash* to life. The flame grows bright reflecting their faces and casting deep shadows on the wall. As he lights the first candle in the *menorah*, the light in the room brightens, and so begins the first night prayers. When he opens his eyes, they become transfixed on the candle and he is back where he lived with his parents on the outskirts of a small village in Poland:

Our Papa was a poor farmer and made a meagre living growing wheat, hay and vegetables. When Mama wanted to call Papa from the fields for his meal, she would play the fiddle and we clapped and danced to her playing. The sound echoed through the valley and when Papa heard it he knew it was time to come home. He dearly loved listening to our music.

One year, Widow Meyer in the next valley had sent word that she desperately needed hay for her sheep and Papa had agreed to take some to her. It would be the first night of Chanukah and that evening we would light the candles and perhaps receive a present.

Papa took the donkey from the stable, harnessed her to the cart and loaded the hay. It was cold and windy as he set off along the road up the hill and over to the widow's house.

Mama was preparing latke and the house filled with the wonderful smell of food. My mouth watered at the thought of what we would eat that night. Not long after Papa had left it began to snow, and the wind played and danced with the snowflakes before they huddled together to carpet the ground. Mama was becoming concerned. If the snow kept falling it would be hard for Papa to follow the road, and it would soon be dark.

My sister prepared the table with a fresh white cloth and placed the *menorah* in the centre with the candles and matches.

It grew dark and late. Papa should have been back long before now, and Mama knew he would be struggling to find his way. She lifted her shawl to cover her head and opened the door. The wind and snow swirled in the light of the open door as Mama peered through the blinding snow and listened intently. But there was nothing. She waited a moment longer, then came back into the house. She asked us to make sure the fire was stoked—he would be so cold when he returned—and we left the curtains open so Papa could see the light.

It grew much later. By now we should have lit the first candle, but not without Papa. Then Mama had an idea.

"Quickly, put on our coats and scarves and come outside on the porch", she told us. She started playing her fiddle, and we all joined in singing, clapping and dancing, raising our voices louder than we had ever sung to carry our music along the sound of the wind. However, even with Mama's playing, and our singing, dancing and clapping it soon became too cold to bear, and she sadly gathered us back into the warmth of the room. Her face was anxious as she picked up the matches and handed them to me to light the *Shamash*.

Just as I was about to slowly strike the match, the door burst open and Papa fell to the floor. Mama rushed to hug him. He had become lost off the road but had struggled on blinded by the swirling snow, when the sound of Mama's playing and our singing guided him in the right direction.

When he had warmed himself by the fire, we stood silently in the darkened room. Embers from the fire cast a reddish shadow on the ceiling as Papa handed me the box and I struck a match to light the *Shamash*.

I passed the light to him and he lit the first candle of Chanukah, the light grew bright, shining on the joy and happiness in our faces.

We thanked God that night for the miracle of Chanukah, and the best present of all—the miracle that brought Papa home to us.

Unlocking more
festive season memories

Do you look forward to the festive season? Why?

Which was the best Christmas you remember? Why?

What is most important about this day for you?

Is it a time of family fun or arguments?

Did you ever visit Santa? Was it in a store, grotto, street or tent?

Can you remember how you felt at the time: excited, scared?

Did you ever pull Santa's beard? How did he react?

Were you taken to watch a Christmas procession? Was it exciting to watch?

Did you help make decorations: lanterns, streamers or paper chains?

Did you put up a Christmas tree? Was it live or artificial?
Did you help dress the tree?

What presents did you buy for mum and dad?

What did you do on Christmas Day or on Chanukah?

Did you play games? Did you attend church or synagogue?

Was the building decorated? How?

Did you take part in a nativity play or sing in a choir?

Did you ever go carol singing? In the street or at neighbours?

Did you ever kiss under the mistletoe? Who with? Did you enjoy it?

How does Christmas or Chanukah today differ from your childhood?

Were there influences from another culture in your childhood celebrations?

Days out and nights to remember

Punch and Judy, I spy, the last waltz,
Old Spice and blue suede shoes.

Did you frequently have family days out? Who with? Do you remember them with fondness?

Days out didn't happen too often when I was little. The industrial city in which we lived was choked with smoke from the mills and from the row upon row of coal-fire burning terrace houses. Fortunately, there were easily accessible moorlands and beauty spots surrounding the city and a day out was an inexpensive family occasion. On the local moors, there were remnants of Roman roads and Druid's circles that combined history and my imagination into living reality.

Mum and Dad also favoured museums and art galleries and at the time I often wished we were going somewhere more interesting, but I now recall those days as ones of pleasurable learning.

If the day out was at the seaside, it was about a sixty mile journey and took us around three hours in a bus that meandered through narrow lanes and by-ways and stopped at pretty villages.

Did you go on games or rides?

At the seaside, sixpence got us a ride on a donkey or a seat at a Punch and Judy show while Mum and Dad paddled in the sea with stockings off and trouser legs rolled up. I used to laugh watching people paddling in three piece suits, topped off with a handkerchief, tied at each corner, to keep the sun off balding heads. After their paddle, Mum and Dad sat on hired deck chairs listening to the Salvation Army brass band. Dad inevitably fell asleep during this relaxed state, his mouth falling open, his false teeth dropping down, and his loud snores accompanying *Jesus wants me for a sunbeam*.

Did you play games or sing songs on the journey? What were they?

Games and songs filled our journey time. I spy with my little eye, was a great favourite and renditions of *Ten green bottles*, *One man went to Mow* and *There were ten in a bed and the little one said roll over,* kept us occupied for most of the journey.

Did you ever go to a fairground? What rides did you like best? Did you win anything? What did you eat at the fair?

Dad loved taking us to Hull Fair, boasted to be the largest in England. It was too big for any municipal park so it was set up in residential streets, leaving only a narrow pavement between the terrace houses and fair stalls. Brandy snaps, toffee apples, and fairy floss stalls were on every corner. We gazed in fascination at the side shows of bearded ladies, half man/half woman (for adults only), and motor cycle riders who rode round and round a wooden cylindrical stage performing death defying tricks. Some enterprising householders rented their front rooms to the numerous fortune tellers, most of whom claimed to be the "original Gypsy Smith".

Did you ever go to a fairground? What rides did you like best? Did you win anything? What did you eat at the fair?

One time, we had been on a day outing, and that night Dad asked if we would like to go to the "blanket market". When we eagerly answered yes, he took us up to bed. That's what blanket market was. He thought it was a great joke.

When we were tucked up, Dad would tell my brother David and me a story. Usually it had something to do with what had happened that day, with the two of us as characters in the story. We nudged each other and giggled until we fell asleep, somehow never hearing the end of the stories.

As teenagers, how did you dress up for your night out? Which night were you "allowed" out?

As a teenager, probably the most exciting day of the week was Friday or Saturday. Preening and dressing up was all part of the ritual, not that we had Armani suits or Christian Dior dresses, but it was about the basic instinct of attracting the opposite sex.

Remember When…

Did girls wear make up or wear perfume? How did you set your hair? Did men wear after shave or cologne?

Girls who worked at the mills set their hair in rollers on Friday mornings, covering their head with a scarf for work. It saved precious time getting ready when they got home and had to prepare for their night out.

The lads polished their shoes, applied Brylcreem to their hair, put on a clean shirt and tie, anointed their cheeks with a handful of Old Spice and, with a neatly folded hanky in the top jacket pocket, were ready for whatever the night would bring. A comb was a necessary piece of equipment for minor touches to the quiff if a mirror or shop window reflected a hair out of place.

For me, girls with bouffant hair dos were a no-no. Not for me the girls who complained if I'd so much as touch or ruffle their stiffened lacquered hair.

Did you meet your dates or call for them?

I never two-timed a girl, though perhaps I did go out with them once and never call again if another came on the scene. I never stood a girl up, and if an arrangement had been made, I would always stick to it even if it meant waiting an hour in snow, ice and sub zero temperatures for a girl who never turned up.

How much did it cost at the cinema? Did the boy pay for the girl, or did you go "Dutch"? Did you sit in the back seats to cuddle your partner?

One night a week, I went to the cinema. It cost a shilling. The back seats were doubles, perfect for snogging, and I never really knew what the film was about. It was just a place to be warm, comfortable and secluded, and by the end of the film our lips were swollen from kissing!

Films were shown as continuous performances, which meant you could walk in at the middle of the film and sit in the cinema until you caught up. It never seemed to matter that you watched the ending before the beginning because it meant you could stay as long as you wanted—a great benefit if you were with a girl you liked.

Did you learn ballroom dancing? Which step did you prefer? Often girls would dance together and be split by two boys. Did this happen to you?

Saturday night was for dancing and socialising. I learned the quickstep, one-two-together, but because of my lack of skill they also became the same steps for a waltz or a foxtrot, only slower. I was much better at creative jive and made a real exhibition of myself dancing with two girls at once. Old time dancing was still popular but Bill Haley and the Comets changed the whole nature of popular music with *Rock around the Clock*. When Elvis Presley sang *Blue Suede Shoes*, rock and roll was here to stay.

Big bands and orchestras played at the larger dance halls with a mixture of old time, swing music and jive. The last waltz was a great smooching conclusion. It was popular with most people at the dance, so there was only room to shuffle around very slowly, arms draped about each other. Nevertheless, it was still romantic.

How did you get home? Were you ever late? What were the consequences?

When a dance finished late and the buses had stopped running, it was a taxi home if you could afford one. By Saturday night my pocket money had usually been spent, so more often than not we walked home.

What was your reaction to the first party you went to?

When I came to Australia, all the girls would sit or stand at one side of the dance floor with the boys at the other side. I had never known this in England. It seemed harder to ask a girl for a dance, especially if she said no and you had to walk back with everyone knowing your request was refused. It really deflated the ego, and the confidence.

Did you ever make a faux pas at a party? What happened?

The first time I was invited to a party in Australia we were asked to take a plate. I thought it very strange, but I did as I had been asked, arriving at the party with a plate neatly tucked under my arm. I thought it was to save washing up. Fortunately, my hosts saw it as a great joke. In future my plates always had food on them.

Unlocking more memories of days out

Where was your favourite place for a day out?

Who did you go with?

What did you enjoy most about your day out?

What did you wear?

What fashion was your swimming costume? Was the material wool?

Which day out was your most memorable?

How much pocket money did you get to spend?

What would you buy on your day out?

Unlocking more memories of memorable nights

Who did you go with on your nights out?

Where was your usual night out venue?

Is there a night you will always remember? What happened?

How did you get home after a late night out: bus, taxi, walking?

Was there a curfew time you had to be home by?

Were you ever late?

Were your parents waiting up?

What were the consequences?

Difficulties and hard times

Faith, hope and the price of bread.

Most people have confronted difficulties or hard times in their life experiences. A hard time may not necessarily be about money, though bringing up families on low wages was difficult for many people, but they survived. Difficulties are often overcome through tenacity, faith and purpose, and that is where there is a story: how overcoming difficulties or hard times made you a stronger person, and how it has affected your philosophy of life today.

What difficulty or hard times do you remember most for you or your family? Did you learn something you value today from the experience you gained? What was it?

My parents had agreed that my mother would always be at home when we returned from school so my father was the only wage earner. He brought home the princely sum of £3.15.00 a week to feed, clothe and house a family of seven, and his wage remained the same for fifteen years. My elder brother remembers not having any money to buy a loaf of bread, but we were better off than some.

My mother kept records of her expenditure from the time she got married. It is interesting, looking at her housekeeping books, how some costs in those days, were often more expensive, pro rata, than today.

How did you cope emotionally with the difficulties and hard times? Did anyone help you? Who helped and how?

Without doubt, it was my mother's religious faith that helped her through the hard times. She often counted her blessings that, except for the usual measles and chicken pox, we were all healthy—though boils and carbuncles reflected our lack of food vitamins until well after the War.

Did gardening or another pastime help overcome your difficulties?

We were fortunate to have a garden where we could grow common vegetables, rhubarb and raspberries to help stretch the budget. Others who did not have a garden could rent an allotment for a couple of shillings a week. Allotments became coveted plots, frequently used as a respite from life's difficulties and lovingly laboured over far into the late twilight of summer evenings.

Did you have a plan to overcome problems, or confront each one as it came along?

For many years, Mum often lay awake worrying how to pay a bill, or how to get the washing machine repaired. She lived until she was ninety-eight and I'm glad to say she received back a comfortable "twilight" from her children. It was small compensation in return for her gift of love and dedication that allowed us to discover our places in life.

Unlocking more memories of difficulties and hard times

How did you manage to survive on a daily basis?

Do you still count your pennies?

Are you still thrifty with food and clothing?

Do you put aside money for a rainy day?

How did the problems affect your family unit?

Have you any advice you would share with your own family or others about your experiences?

Faith, spirituality and superstition

Fellowship, the Pope's telephone, Billy Graham and leprechauns.

How did religion play a part in your childhood or family?

My religion as a child was Methodist, with attendance three times every Sunday: junior church, led by my mother on Sunday morning; then afternoon Sunday school; a family service in the evening; and sometimes Sunday youth fellowship. Not surprisingly, we knew all the rousing popular hymns of John Wesley by heart.

Chapel and Methodism were a great part of our social life. Concerts and plays, picnics and field days, Christmas parties, scouts, cubs, brownies and guides all made for a wonderfully active life. However, young questioning minds did not always receive a constructive or logical answer from our clergy. I questioned why the portrayal of Christ on a picture in the Sunday school, represented him with smooth white skin, blonde hair and blue eyes, and wearing a Persil washed white robe. My small mind questioned that if he were a carpenter, he would have been very masculine with big rough hands, just like Mr. Close the joiner in the village.

I never received a satisfactory answer.

Do you still practise a religion? Is it different from the one taught to you as a child? How does it differ?

I was "saved" three times by the emotional summons of the evangelist, Billy Graham. His call to accept Christ seemed to trigger my feelings of guilt and sin and, to the choral strains of *Just as I am without one plea*, I willingly responded to his call. I knew I would wake to a new world the next morning, different to any other. But somehow the difference seemed to evade me, and eventually the call to Christ faded. I lived my life without further religious persuasion.

My father used to write to the Pope to ask why he had a gold telephone at his bedside. If he sold it, the money would feed many of the hungry people in poor countries. I don't think he received an answer.

Have you ever experienced religious wars or bigotry?

Religious "wars" can rage at the local level too. In our village, the local Fagley Roman Catholics didn't seem to like those who did not pursue the "one true religion". They equipped themselves with dustbin lids as shields and, wielding sticks, they came in search of disbelievers. Their priest never interfered, and we in turn fought back with a great deal of guilt. Somewhere there was a misconception—a breakdown—between religion and love.

How did superstitions affect you as a child? Do they still affect you today? How do they affect you?

The history and folklore of Ireland has been married to superstition from the Celts to present day. I met Trish Daly, a lovely Irish colleen with a distinct Irish brogue, when she organised my holiday travel arrangements. Her small cottage has all the little reminders of the old country with photographs of places and family adorning the walls. Her picture book garden includes an Irish quotation carved in stone, and you half expect to see "the little people" coming out to play when all is quiet.

As a child, Trish Daly recalls her absolute belief in leprechauns. They were as real, she says, as the rainbow painted in the sky after a storm and the common belief that there was always a crock of gold waiting at the end (if you could find the rainbow's end).

Fear also propagated superstition and, like many children and adults at that time, Trish feared the Banshee, the terrible taker of life. It seemed to her the church did little to dismiss the superstitions that haunted so many souls, for it kept people embracing

Christianity out of fear, but as Trish grew older, an enquiring mind eventually dispelled the Banshee, and her fear was forgotten.

Unlocking more memories of faith, spirituality and superstitions

Was there a time in your life, faith played a significant role? For example during periods of war, struggle, loss, suffering or imprisonment?

How did your faith help you?

Did you attend worship regularly with your family or alone?

Did you have Sunday best or festival clothes to wear? Describe them.

What beliefs are still important to you?

Do your beliefs differ from those of your parents? How? Why?

Do you or any family members have any little superstitions they act upon?

Do you read astrology charts? Can you remember anything significant that ever came true?

Have you ever been to a fortune-teller? What did she foretell? Was her prophecy accurate?

Family characters

Auntie Nell, uncle Willie and Hitler's moustache.

Did your family have any characters or eccentrics? Did you or the family embrace, or reject them? Why?

I had a wonderfully eccentric great aunt Nell who lived seventy miles from us at Hull, in east Yorkshire. There were not enough beds at her house so when we stayed with her I had to sleep in a drawer.

Aunt Nell put on a posh voice whenever we visited. She put an "h" on words like apple so it would become "happle" with emphasis on the "h". I thought it hilarious but had to cover my laughter because I didn't want her to think I was rude. When she smoked after a meal, she puffed her smoke under the tablecloth so it wouldn't offend anybody. I loved what she did.

I had an uncle Willie, Dad's brother who fought in the trenches of northern France during the First World War. He was very slightly built and sported a Hitler type moustache. Except for rare outings to weddings or funerals when he dressed up in a beautiful three-piece suit, he'd wear a detached collar shirt (tunic shirt), and a well worn waistcoat and trousers. Uncle Willie had suffered gas poisoning and had great difficulty breathing, but it didn't stop him smoking his Woodbines continuously, and every so often give a wrenching cough. I would watch in wonder as the wet and tobacco stained cigarette in his mouth was rolled from side to side while he quietly hummed and poked the fire. The humming was not in tune with anything known or recognised and he would occasionally interrupt himself by asking if Mum and Dad were well, or if David was still at the School of Art. There was never much conversation, but he liked us to go and see him.

Grandmother Hockney was very deaf and, though not quite blind, had very poor vision because of cataracts. When my brother Paul visited her she opened the door, peered at him and asked, "Who's there?" He would answer, "It's Paul". Then she'd turn round and shout to uncle Willie, "It's the coal".

When I went to visit her, Grandma would say, "I'll just change my dress and she'd reappear minutes later with another dress over the one she was already wearing. She had a cataract operation when she was eighty-nine and after that she completely redecorated the house, began using make-up, and wore her clothes with great distinction. Her renewed sight made such a difference to her—she became quite the lady.

My grandparents, on my mother's side, were early members of The Salvation Army. Grandad was a captain, and Grandma a lieutenant. When they fell in love, the Salvation Army would not approve of the marriage unless Grandad relinquished his rank as captain. They decided no one would dictate the conditions of their marriage, so they both left the Salvation Army for the Bradford Methodist Mission, where they continued their work helping the poor and homeless. Grandad also hawked old furniture and eventually, after studying, became an antique dealer.

Did you visit your grandparents often? Did they tell you stories?

Unlocking more memories of extended family and family characters

What do you remember most about your grandparents?

Did they live close by or with you?

How often did you see them?

What clothes did they wear?

What sort of work did they do?

How did they meet? Where did they get married?

Are family photos of the wedding available?

Did they buy their own home or rent?

What sort of transport did they use to go to work or to go on holidays?

Was there a sense and feeling of real loss when they passed away?

Were you close to any aunts and uncles? When did you see them?

Where did they live? What sort of work did they do?

Did you ever stay over, or go on a trip with them?

Were there any black sheep in the family? What had they done? Did you meet them?

Did you have "adopted" aunties or uncles who were close to you as a child?

Did you grow up with cousins?

Did you frequently see or play with them?

Did you have common interests? Did you holiday together?

Did you mind sharing things with each other?

Do you still keep in touch?

Family (immediate)

Union Jack socks, lip reading and *Wed Wiver Valley*.

Where did your parents meet? How long did they court?

My parents were both Sunday school teachers, and Dad was also a local preacher. They knew each other by sight, but it was not until an outing to Bolton Abbey that they began to court each other. They married in 1929. Mum was thirty, Dad twenty-six.

What were they like as parents?

Mum worked hard in the family home and made sure her children knew how to fend for themselves. By the time we were twelve we could all cook a roast dinner and iron shirts and dresses.

As Dad's hearing worsened, he no longer enjoyed conversation and socialising. Instead, he became a one-man protest parade with banners unfurled in support of any worthwhile cause—and never heard the rebukes from passers by.

What was the worst part of having brothers and sisters? What was the best part? Did you have a good relationship with them?

My brothers and sister were fun, interesting, knowledgeable and great teasers. I had difficulty pronouncing my "Rs", and my brothers, Paul and Philip especially, would mock me by singing *Wed Wiver Valley* with loud gusto. I was an easy catch.

In 1977, Paul became Lord Mayor of Bradford and during his inaugural mayoral procession, raised his leg over the side of his open carriage proudly displaying his Union Jack socks. Later, Bradfordians responded to the Lord Mayor's Charity Appeal by knitting thousands of Union Jack socks.

My second brother, Philip, emigrated to Australia in 1963 with his family as "Ten Pound Poms". He designed road petrol tankers, and his dream was to one day have his own business. He achieved his wish, and with the design of a tanker with a lower (much safer) centre of gravity, he even exported them back to England.

My sister, Margaret, has a very analytical mind and was always a wizard at solving puzzles. She was a highly qualified (and awarded) nurse and for a while worked in a leper colony and in the General Hospital in Zambia. When the family affliction of poor hearing worsened to the point where she had to learn to lip read, she studied for six years to become a naturopath and ran a small but successful practice until her ever-failing hearing again stopped her. Undaunted, she learnt the computer and even set up a web design school. She has since developed techniques for creating pictures of flowers and has a modest but growing demand for her artwork.

My brother David was closest in age to me. We played together, shared an attic bedroom together and shared some of the same friends. Even as a young boy, it was apparent he had a special artistic talent, but in the early post war years the blank white edges of newspapers and magazines were the only spaces he could practise his drawing and sketching skills.

He lived very frugally as a student so he could buy paint and canvases, and managed to get financial assistance from small council or government grants, delivering bread, or from casual jobs on farms.

He was a very likeable fellow and had many friends. He stood out, not just for his artistic abilities, but also for his outspoken concerns about injustice. Even in his early teenage years, David had an ability to reason and a vocabulary to choose his words wisely.

His art reflects a continuous pursuit of knowledge and discovery—the legacy our parents passed on to all of us.

Unlocking more close family memories

Did your father ask your mother's parents for her hand in marriage?

Did they marry in a religious or civil ceremony?

Where did they marry? Did they elope?

Did they have a honeymoon?

Have you any stories of their courting days or early marriage?

Where did they live? Was their home close to their parents?

Did they rent a house or buy their own?

Did they own a car—or some other form of transport? What was it?

Are family photos available to use in your story?

How many brothers and sisters did you have? What were the age differences between you? What position in the family were you?

If you were an only child, did you long for a brother or sister?

What was the worst part of being an only child?

What was the best part of being an only child?

What work did your brothers/sisters do when they left school?

Did you get on with your brothers/sisters?

Did you go to the same school together?

Do you still see or contact your brothers/sisters?

Did you have to share a room? Did you have to share a bed?

Did you have to wear hand-me-down clothing?

What was your favourite game with the family?

Were any of you musical or otherwise creative?

Do you have any interests with your siblings, other than family interest? What are they?

Do you share the same sense of humour or mannerisms?

Festivals and festivities

Shamrocks, *crostoli*, Morris men
and Catherine wheels.

IRISH FESTIVALS

The Irish are a special people. Though their history is rife with the tragedies of famine, war and oppression there is always room for a smile, a song and a celebration. Trish Daly shared some of her childhood memories and, in particular, St Patrick's Day.

How did you celebrate St. Patrick's Day as a child? How do you celebrate it now? Did you participate in a street parade? What part did you play?

The day is part spiritual, part celebratory, and family preparations started a week beforehand with the search for fresh shamrocks to wear to mass. The tiny plant has a place in the heart of the Irish people not only as a symbol of freedom, but also because St Patrick used the three leaves of the shamrock to represent the Trinity when he began preaching Christianity. The popular St Patrick's mass is followed by a lively street parade with costumed dancers, Irish traditional music and lots of fun. A huge roast dinner was prepared for family and guests, older members partook in a drop or two, and the children delightedly watched the frivolity.

For Trish, the day was always more special when her cousins from the United States visited. One time they brought huge round badges to wear, with "Kiss me I'm Irish" emblazoned in large letters, a reminder that celebrations in America differed somewhat from those in the homeland.

Do you still celebrate St Patrick's Day?

Since living in Australia, Trish feels St Patrick's Day is more important to her than it was in Ireland. Irish people love coming together on St Patrick's Day and Trish enjoys the recognition of national identity no matter where she happens to be. It's a day when strangers meet, share stories, quench their dry throats with Guinness or Irish whiskey, and join in to sing beloved Irish songs with newfound friends.

ITALIAN FESTIVALS

Lucia d'Allesandra from Italy, fondly remembers celebrating the Easter festival, Buona Pasqua.

How did you celebrate the Easter *carnavale*? What food did you eat? Who prepared the food? Did you join a street parade? Did you dress up, play an instrument or dance? What did you wear?

On Easter Sunday, before the special mass, the whole town assembled at the monument to honour the dead. After mass it was home with the whole family: cousins, aunties, uncles and grandma to share a mouth-watering baked lamb.

On Easter Monday, the family busied themselves preparing food for a huge picnic. This was the day that new outfits were worn—it was springtime and new life was being born. Games were played, there was lots to eat, and wine to drink—mixed with a little water or lemonade for the children. A special treat always eaten at *carnavale* was *crostoli*, a dough mixture in the shape of a bow, deep fried to a crispy case, then sprinkled with sugar.

What Lucia loved most was dressing up—only ever as a fairy—and joining her cousins, friends and other children in a procession through the town, winding through the narrow streets towards the castle until they met Dama Bianca the lady ghost of the castle. Wide eyed, open-mouthed, and in absolute belief that she was real, the children watched the ghost appear and disappear.

BRITISH FESTIVALS

How did you celebrate May Day? How was the day celebrated?

May Day in England is a beautiful, colourful festival celebrating the coming of summer, and dating back to medieval times.

May Day is also a time for lovers and, in Eccleshill, the village where I lived, the May Day king and queen were selected from local courting couples. Children and young people danced around the maypole interweaving with the coloured ribbons, and exchanged simple presents of flowers.

The village houses were decorated with flowers and tree branches, their sweet aroma wafting through the air.

We decorated bicycles, scooters or prams with bright coloured crepe paper and took part in a procession through the village behind the May Day king and queen. Traditional songs and dances were then performed in the village square or a nearby field.

In some villages, there was folk dancing by Morris Men who wore white shirts and trousers, black-buckled shoes with bells on, and brightly coloured hats with feathers. Their dances were very energetic. Legs and arms flayed in the air in perfect body unison, while arms wielded long sticks with bright coloured ribbons and bells.

We thought it wonderful that history gave us Guy Fawkes who had tried to blow up the Houses of Parliament one November 5. It provided an excuse to celebrate his foiled plot with fireworks and a bonfire.

At least a month beforehand, neighbourhood kids began to drag tree branches or old palings towards a carefully selected site to build the best and biggest bonfire. "Progging" or "chumping" we called it. An effigy of Guy Fawkes was perched in an old armchair carefully positioned on the top of the bonfire.

It was dark early in November, so at about six o'clock the fire was lit and flames quickly began to lick the outside timbers like darting fingers pushing up to reach the Guy. When the Guy started to burn we always cheered loudly. We stood around the fire, our faces and fronts glowed with warmth, but our backs froze.

Which fireworks did you enjoy most?

Most parents preferred rockets, spin wheels, Catherine wheels and rainbow fountains, but we kids preferred the noise of crackers and thunderbolts. Old rope, salvaged from the local woollen mills, was saturated with wool grease and cut into foot-long pieces. Lit at one end they made a perfect, long-lasting taper for lighting our fireworks.

What did you have to eat? What did you enjoy most?

Mushy peas, hot cocoa, "parkin pigs" and cinder toffee kept us warm inside as the fire slowly subsided to a red and white-hot glow. Potatoes were pushed into the embers until they began to blacken on the outside. We ate them—burning our tongues—with butter dribbling down the sides. Potatoes never taste quite the same as those cooked in the bonfire.

LEBANESE FESTIVALS

The Birth of The Prophet is the cultural festival Souad Daizli enjoys most. The festival, celebrating the birth of Mohammed, is a time to be joyful. Families and neighbours work together in preparing for the day, and colourful decorations adorn homes and streets. A wonderful variety of sweets and pastries are made, which have to contain something white such as milk or yoghurt. White represents purity and peace, and is an essential part of the celebration.

Unlocking more festival and festivities memories

What memories do you have of festivals and festivities?

Were they religious, political or military celebrations?

Which country did you live in then?

Did you celebrate at home with family?

Were you expected to watch the celebrations?

Do you remember your first bonfire and fireworks?

Did you or anyone you know have an accident with fireworks?

Have you ever seen a big firework display?

How did you feel watching the sky burst into colours?

Do you actively participate in a national day celebration?

How do you participate and with whom?

Do you wear something traditional or special? What does it look like?

What is the most important festive day in the year for you? Why?

Food we used to eat

Bread and dripping, frog spawn, tzimmes and spotted Dick.

Was your food ever rationed? What was your staple diet?

We seemed to survive on bread and dripping during the War and into the 1940s and 50s. It tasted scrumptious with a sprinkling of salt. We walked or cycled a lot, not necessarily by design but out of necessity, so I think we soon got rid of the fats. There were very few fat people in those days.

What did you like most about your mother's cooking?

Mum was a vegetarian so she received extra cheese, butter and nuts through her ration book. She used to make a wonderful cheese pudding as a main course. It was a bread and butter pudding recipe but with cheese and onion mixed into the bread. I can still smell the aroma and imagine the taste.

We often had homemade potted meat or fish paste sandwiches, lots of suet puddings and dumplings made with suet in a stew. "Spotted Dick" with currants and raisins served with custard was a family favourite, or apple and blackberry pudding made with fresh fruit picked from local hedgerows.

Was there any food you really longed for but couldn't have?

There was a famous pie shop in Bradford called Roberts. The shop front was painted brown, except for a small window area at eye level and—no matter what time of day—the window displayed a large crusty pie cooked to a perfect golden brown. You could tell the pie was still hot by the steam escaping through a small hole in the centre of the crust. For me, the pie always remained just a mouth watering distant wish.

Remember When...

Did you have school dinners? What sort of menu was offered?

Hot school dinners were introduced during the War. They cost two pence, and meant every child got a hot meal at least once a day. If parents couldn't afford the cost, their child received dinners free of charge. Menus were quite static and repetitious: brown Windsor soup, mince with mashed potatoes and vegetables, followed by sago pudding. Sago was known as frog spawn and not many kids liked it, but I loved it, so was happy to get seconds and thirds.

What do you recall from family get togethers? How old were you? What food do you remember eating? Did you have a favourite?

My friend and associate storyteller, Donna Jacobsife, has vivid memories of Seder night and food at her aunt's house during her childhood. She writes:

I remember the long table taking up all the space in the room so that it was a major strategic achievement to get all the family seated. Only the ones carefully placed at the ends of the table could get up to help serve the great plates of roast chicken, matzahball soup, sweet and sour beans, potato kugel, and tzimmes: soul food, food I knew from somewhere inside myself as remnants of a past world.

The dining room had a small frosted window that always remained ajar. While the others sang of freedom and prophets, I, the dreamer of the family, stared at the window imagining that all Jews out there were doing this. I came from the non-believing, non-kosher side of the family and the thought gave me great comfort. It wrapped me in the knowledge of something greater, something beyond.

Do you create recipes from memory? Do the recipes taste as you remember them? Is there a difference? Can you identify the difference?

When I grew up and became a mother, I wanted to recreate those soul food moments for my children. One year, just before Rosh Hashanah, I started to remember the taste of tzimmes.

It had been a long time since I had eaten my auntie's tzimmes but I went to the supermarket and bought carrots and prunes, took them home, and experimented. The first attempt was too dry. The next, not sweet enough, not thick enough. There was a particular quality that I was trying to find. During one attempt, I turned the oven down to very low and then forgot about it, and went to bed. When I awoke the next morning there was a smell that filled the house. It was a smell that evoked something very powerful in my memory. That was it. That was the quality I could not describe, but knew was missing. The result was a rich and thick dish, dark in colour, and heavy with meaning.

But that is not the end of the story. A couple of years after the great tzimmes discovery, I visited my auntie just after Passover. She had some leftover tzimmes in the fridge and asked if I wanted some. Of course I did. However the taste was nothing like I remembered. I asked if she had changed the recipe. She said she had not.

"But are these the same tzimmes you would serve at Seder when I was little?" I asked.

She insisted she hadn't changed the recipe for forty years.

It was a mystery. We agreed to meet the following week and I would bring her some of my tzimmes. I thought they would remind her that, long ago, she really did make a different tzimmes. At the appointed time, I arrived with my little plastic container. We sat down together. I watched her carefully as she raised the fork to her lips and chewed ponderously. Then, I was astonished to see her eyes fill with tears. She leaned forward, put her hand on my arm and said, "Donna-le. This is the tzimmes my mother used to make."
Her mother—my grandmother—had died when I was five. Somehow, it was that taste, that quality I had remembered and tried so hard to reproduce.

Soul food. What else would you call it?

Unlocking more food memories

What items were always kept in your pantry?

How has food (and storing food) changed from your childhood?

What did you most like about your mother's cooking?

What did you dislike most about your mother's cooking?

Could your father cook?

Did you learn to cook at school? What did you cook or bake?

Did your mother teach you to cook? What did you make?

Do you still make a dish taught to you by your mother? What is it?

Were you ever treated to eat at a restaurant or café as a child? Where was it? What did you eat? Was it a special occasion?

Did you have a garden or allotment to grow your own vegetables?

If you could have your favourite childhood dish today, what would it be?

How were left overs served up?

What was your favourite mouth watering smell of cooking?

Which foods do you remember for any festival days you celebrated?

What did you enjoy most about the festivals?

Have you continued the traditions?

Has the food changed?

Friends and neighbours

Vicars, tramps and street parties.

Do you have many long term friends?

I have gathered many friends over the years, but those from my infant school and high school days are very special. We grew up together, and came from the same socio-economic background. I still see them whenever I visit England or they come to Australia.

Have you lost friends in tragedy or illness? Describe your feelings at that time?

A true friend, who totally accepts who you are, warts and all, is to be treasured. Most of my long term friends are still alive, but my older brother, David, has lost so many to tragedy and illness over the years.

My mother lived to ninety-eight, and all her friends and family passed on before she did. Without the support of friends, it can become a lonely time of life.

How well did you know your neighbours? Did you help each other?

People didn't move house frequently and local families knew each other well. Most neighbours were friendly and looked after each other, and everyone called each other, "luv". It was never a problem borrowing a cup of sugar, flour or milk.

There was a sense of security provided by the regular "bobbies" (policemen) who patrolled on foot through the village. We were brought up with the knowledge that if we were in trouble, talk to a policeman and they would help. They did!

Did you have street parties with your neighbours? What were the celebrations?

There were the street parties and annual festivals, like May Day and bonfire night, when the whole street made sandwiches and cakes and decorated the street with flags and bunting.

When we were old enough to have a pint in the local, we created our fun by dressing up and going to a new pub where we weren't known. Two of us might choose to dress as vicars (with waistcoats turned backwards and detached collars turned around) others dressed as tramps or farm hands. By entering the pub at different times no one, supposedly, knew we were together. We would sit close by each other, and talk loudly on whatever subject or scheme we had planned, making sure others could overhear the conversation. The vicars discussed their recent visit to the archbishop and, on observing the tramps, offered them a free pint of ale before going on their way. We got a great kick out of the comments people made on our kindness and generosity, and marvelled at how they believed our harmless scam.

Sometimes we decided on a French, German, Russian or Italian accent and practised for days. Once outside the pub we usually doubled-up with laughter at our own silliness. It was pure theatre and we had a lot of fun.

Unlocking more memories of friends and neighbours

Do you still have friends from your schooldays? Do you still see or write to them?

Do you have any letters from childhood friends? How has life changed since then? How long have you known them? What similar interests do you share?

Who is/was your best lifelong friend? Where did you meet?

Do you have you a special friend you can share your innermost thoughts with?

Was your best friend a bridesmaid/best man at your wedding?

Could you always take friends home?

Did your parents always like your friends?

Do you continue to make new friends?

Holidays

Camping, guesthouses and donkey rides.

What did you do in school holidays?

For me, holidays bring back memories of long hot English summers and six weeks away from school with lots of new adventures to embark on. The family always spent one week at Hull or Withernsea on the east coast of Yorkshire. We stayed at great aunt Nell's, and to get there we had to take the red West Yorkshire bus to Leeds then change to the dark blue and cream East Yorkshire buses. To me the colour difference of the buses was very exciting, and if it was a double decker bus there was a scramble to be first up the stairs. There was so much more to see sitting on the top deck.

What sort of activities did you join in on holiday? Which city, resort or country did you or your family visit for your annual holiday?

We made daily trips from aunt Nell's across the River Humber on the ferry from Hull to New Holland, then took the train to Cleethorpes. Dad loved this area, referring to it as having the most bracing air in England. Cleethorpes faced the North Sea and had a small pebbly beach where we children could play while the grown ups sat in deck chairs rugged up in overcoats and scarves (this was summer, after all).

The Hockney family originated from around Withernsea by the sea, about twelve miles from Hull and we often went back there during the summer holidays. One of the only entertainments in this small village was a visit to distant relatives where we were greeted with awkward smiles and forced conversation. After a cup of tea we beat a hasty retreat, our duty done for another year.

What did you do at home during the holidays?

We had to make our own fun. I never remember being bored at home. We'd be up early and off to the local beauty spots or to a museum or ancient abbey. We walked or cycled everywhere—if we hadn't, we'd never have gone anywhere.

My sister, Margaret, and I loved to walk the seven miles along the canal embankment to Kirkstall Abbey. The two of us never stop talking, discovering birds nests in hedges or watching a barge pass by on its way to Liverpool. The bargees were similar to gypsies but with a home on the water. In my childish fantasy I envied them, but in reality I suspect their pace of life would have bored me.

Did you ever have a camping holiday? Where did you go? Was it comfortable? Were you rained out?

Camping holidays usually meant bitter cold rain and saturated tents until I moved to Australia and discovered new places, new plants and new terrors. I was wary of snakes and spiders and was very happy that our tents had built-in ground sheets and zippered sides to repel the possibility of nightly intruders.

Did you have a special holiday place you loved? Did you go often? Try and describe what it was like, and why you loved it so much?

A favourite place in Australia was the ghost town of Newnes, an old shale oil mining town some forty kilometres down a one-way valley west of the Blue Mountains. The only building left standing was the pub. The resident landlord, Jim Gale, was born there when the town was still booming. Jim served only bottled beer and soft drinks, and would open as long as there were customers. The quiet of the valley was shattered by the putt putt noise of his generator, but the noise was also a signal to thirsty campers that the pub was open for business.

Further afield, up near the Queensland border, I discovered O'Reilly's guesthouse. It was a twenty-five mile drive from Canungra to Lamington Plateau and, when we arrived, I thought I'd found paradise on earth. To the east was a spectacular view to the Gold Coast, and to the west the New South Wales hinterland with Mount Barney dominating the distant skyline.

Bernard O'Reilly was the founder of the guesthouse and was famous for finding the Stinson aircraft that had crashed over the ranges on its way from Brisbane in 1937. While most people thought the aircraft had flown out to sea, Bernard felt compelled to set off into the bush along the route he had calculated as the plane's flight path. He found the aircraft and saved the lives of two of its occupants. Bernard wrote a fascinating book entitled *Green Mountains and Cullenbong*, telling of the life on Lamington Plateau. Well worth reading.

The O'Reillys encouraged campers to join guests in regular nights of entertainment. Over the many years I visited, I wrote a play for the O'Reilly children and helped entertain guests with songs and stories. One play, especially written for Christmas at O'Reillys, was performed by their children for ten years.

Unlocking more holiday memories

What was the best holiday you ever had in your life? What was the worst?

When you were old enough, did you share a holiday with friends?

Where did you go? What did you do?

Did you ever have a romantic holiday for two? Where did you go and with whom?

What special memories have you of your romantic holiday?

What did you take with you on holidays?

Where did you stay: hotel, guesthouse, boarding house, bed and breakfast?

Was the accommodation comfortable and clean?

What sort of food did you eat?

How much did it cost?

Household chores

Spit and polish, washdays and shoes with bicycle tyres.

Did you or your siblings have to help with household chores? What did you have to do?

In the Hockney household, we had work lists of chores and from an early age we were taught to iron, cook simple food, and became expert in scrubbing pans, washing and drying dishes, none of which I was terribly enthusiastic about.

Twenty-four pairs of shoes had to be cleaned each week with Cherry Blossom boot polish using a soft and hard brush and a soft cloth. To get longer wear out of our shoes Dad repaired and resoled them with old bicycle tyres.

Chores could often be renegotiated with other family members, which led to some not so friendly squabbles about who had not done their bit properly. Usually, I was at the receiving end of these arguments.

Was there a weekly schedule of household chores? What were they?

Terrace houses had stone steps and stone window ledges and it was a common sight to see women on their hands and knees scrubbing the steps, then applying a white or yellow stone soap each end of the step and to the front of the windowsill. A clean "front of house" was a badge of honour in the sooty grimy cities of the north.

Each weekday was an allocated day for particular household chores. Monday was washday, Tuesday was for ironing, Wednesday for mending or sewing, Thursday for cleaning, Friday for shopping and Saturday for baking. Sunday was a day of rest. Then it would start all over again.

During summer we had to hang fly paper off the light fitting. It was a brown gummy paper and when flies landed on it, they stuck to it. The only trouble was, there was no point in removing it until it was full, and by then the flies really began to look quite horrible.

Unlocking more memories of household chores

What equipment did your grandmother and grandfather use for their household chores?

How different were the appliances they used, to those of your mother and father's?

What sort of labour saving appliances did you have in your home?

Is there a chore or method of cooking your mother/father taught you that you still use today? What is it?

Have you taught your children the same chore?

Did you have to make your bed and keep your room tidy as a child?

Did you always do it? What happened if you didn't?

Do you do the same with your children now?

Did you have ways of escaping chores or swapping with your brothers or sisters?

Did your attitude to chores carry through to adulthood?

Were you paid for chores, or was your pocket money dependent on your doing them?

Illness, cures and "looking good"

Mustard baths, cod liver oil, lavender water and Brylcreem.

Did your grandmother or mother have any special remedies you remember?

Mum was a firm believer in fresh air and if we got a cold, she would rug us up and take us for a walk, then tuck us into bed. If the cold got worse, she prepared a mustard bath to open the pores and help sweat out the infection. Most of the "old wives" remedies worked, and even today I still prefer fresh air to sitting or lying in a hot room.

If ever I bumped my head, a kiss from Mum and a lump of butter rubbed into the affected part, would soon dispel the hurt. Cuts and abrasions cleaned with Dettol, and an Elastoplast tenderly placed over the wound, immediately helped to make things better.

Was there much illness in your family? What illnesses did you or your family contract as children: mumps, measles, chickenpox? How did you get well?

Mum didn't believe in keeping us back from school unless we were really ill, though most of us contracted one of the common diseases of the period: whooping cough, mumps, measles or German measles. My sister became ill with scarlet fever, and had to be quarantined at the fever hospital. No one could have contact with her, and Mum and Dad had to observe her progress through a glass window.

Did you have to take preventative medicines?

Because there was a lack of fresh fruit in England during the War, school pupils were given a daily glass of orange juice with cod liver oil. I hated cod liver oil and played truant until I was excused from the dosage. School milk was also provided free to ensure each child received the necessary calcium supplement.

What were the remedies of the day?

Even so, the lack of vitamins in most people's diets made boils and carbuncles commonplace. They were excruciatingly painful, and I remember David screaming in pain as hot kaolin poultices were applied to draw out the puss.

Other more complex diseases such as tuberculosis and polio were rife, and for a smallpox scare in the early sixties, we each had to take an inoculated sugar cube.

The summer heat induced heat spots or a heat rash for which we were given sulphur tablets and calamine lotion. Virol, malt extract, or slippery elm food were also used to help purify the blood.

Where did you get your medications?

We collected nettles in the early summer months (with our gloves on of course) so Mum could brew her wonderfully refreshing nettle beer. Not only did it taste good, the herbal qualities also provided blood purification, so it lessened the risk of heat spots. Where there were nettles there were also dock leaf plants. Their leaves soothed the pain from the stinging nettles.

A display of huge pear-shaped bottles containing bright red, green, purple or blue coloured water was the recognisable symbol of a chemist shop. The chemist mixed medicines into liquid mixtures or tablets while you waited, and prescriptions took a long time before they were ready. At the back of the counter, the wall was covered with small wooden drawers containing hundreds of healing substances, and each drawer was labelled, with its contents sign written in Latin with gold lettering.

What beauty products were used? How often were they worn: once a week, everyday?

In Yorkshire, frequent fine soft rain helped complexions remain "baby's bottom" soft, and the only beauty aid I remember most girls wearing was lipstick.

Even so, there were many recipes for homemade hand and face creams using fruit and plant products. My grandmother was very proud of her smooth skin even when she was old, and used cucumber with glycerine and honey to keep her youthful looks. Pantry shelves always contained rose water, vinegar and olive oil, the basic ingredients for a variety of beauty recipes.

Mum always looked lovely. She very rarely used make up, though this was perhaps through economic deprivation rather than a desire not to enjoy any beauty aids. I once bought her a bottle of lavender water. It was a big bottle embellished with a fake cut-glass finish and contained a purplish liquid. It was only nine pence from Woolworths, and I considered it a wonderful gift. I thought it must have been very precious to her because it stood unused on her dressing table for years. I realised many years later she had never liked it.

Men plastered their hair with Brylcreem, trying hard to imitate the film star image of Clark Gable or Humphrey Bogart.

For special occasions, such as a wedding or funeral, when lady's hair lacquer was unavailable or too expensive, a mixture of water and sugar, boiled into a colourless liquid, fixed their hair into position.

Stockings were scarce or unaffordable so a brown line drawn down the back of the leg gave women the appearance of wearing nylons.

Unlocking more memories of illness/cures/looking good

Do you remember your family doctor?

How much did he charge?

What was the worst tasting medicine you ever had?

Did you have a medicine chest at home? What was in it?

Did you have a school dentist come to check your teeth?

Did a school doctor come to check your health?

Did you have teeth out? With cocaine or gas?

Did they look in your hair (for lice or nits)?

Did you or a family member go to hospital?

What illness did you/they have?

What was the treatment in hospital?

How long were they there?

How many beds were in the ward?

Was it a public or private hospital?

What did the nurses wear?

Was washing your hair a weekly chore?

Which night did you wash your hair?

What soap did you use?

Men, did you shave only for special occasions or every day?

Did you use a safety razor or a cut-throat razor with a leather strop?

Did you wear after-shave lotion? What else did you use?

What was your favourite hairdressing?

Listening and watching

Wireless, soaps, Ed Sullivan, 78s and 45s.

When my mother was five, she could happily play along the tramlines on the street. There were very few cars, and transport for most people was on foot, by bicycle or on buses, trams and trains.

Spaceships to Mars and the moon were just fiction and fantasy stories in boys' comics. Who would have believed the moon would be reached in our lifetime.

How did you make telephone calls? How much did it cost? Was it through an exchange? Did the telephonist listen in?

The first telephones were heavy and clumsy, and calls were directed through an exchange where the operator (always female) listened in to the gossip and private news.

Before Mum and Dad had a phone at home, Dad made-do by using the local phone box up the street—not just to make calls, but to receive them too. The public phone boxes cost twopence a call and when the person answered you had to press button A and the money dropped for payment. If there was no response by pressing button B your twopence was returned… sometimes.

This public phone box was essential to Dad's business during the War when he made dolls' prams to supplement the family income. When he finished a pram, he advertised it in the local newspaper quoting a phone number to ring on a Saturday morning. With a deck chair under one arm, and a daily newspaper in his hand, Dad planted himself outside the local public phone box a few hundred yards up the road. If anyone came to use it, he would simply tell them he was waiting for a special call, and ask if they would mind using the other phone box a short distance up the road. Most people complied or, at most, grudgingly objected but moved on.

It was a source of embarrassment to my mother and she was greatly relieved when we eventually had a phone installed. We were taught to answer the phone politely, always with the number, "Bradford 37919", and never to say our name until we knew who it was.

Which wireless programmes did you/your parents enjoy? Did you all listen together?

The wireless was a piece of furniture, beautifully finished in oak or mahogany, and took pride of place in the living room. I spent hours turning the dial very slowly to pick up foreign stations from out of the static. It was a real thrill to pick up a different language and try to determine which country it was.

Dad and Mum never missed the daily news and, on Christmas Day at 3 pm, everyone had to be silent for the King's speech. We never missed the *Children's Hour*, and Mum's favourite was *Mrs. Dale's Diary* at which time household chores came to a stop.

In the Australian bush, wireless and shortwave radio were essential contacts for remote property owners. It was not just company, but essential for emergencies and schooling. I have twice performed as a storyteller at School of the Air in Broken Hill, and the kids had to have both hands on the transmission equipment so instead of clapping after a story, I heard a chorus of "coo-ee" as an affirmative response back to base. It remains a very special memory.

Do you recall the first TV you watched?

The first televisions were only ten and twelve inch screens, and programmes were broadcast only a few hours each day. Friends were invited around just to watch the small screen moving pictures and anyone whose parents owned a TV suddenly became very popular at school.

Do you have any special memories of the early days of television?

Whether it was part of Dad's eccentricity or just his sense of history in recording special events, he'd set up his still camera in front of our television. He placed a placard on top of the television to identify the historic event and photographed anything he felt important. In the days before home video cameras, when man walked on the moon, he created a photograph of the actual moment Armstrong made the first historic step.

Sporting events, and an interview with Bing Crosby by Ed Sullivan were also favourites—though in the case of the latter, the TV picture had, incongruously, just switched to Louis Armstrong's face by the time Dad had written out his placard and clicked the camera shutter. His scrapbooks of these photographs are now family treasures.

Did you have a wind up gramophone? Who were your favourite singers or bands on the old "78" records?

Wind up gramophones played ten inch and twelve inch discs that were very brittle and had very poor sound quality. Nevertheless, the thrill of hearing music through a funnel was exciting, and we lay on the floor listening to scratchy jazz and shrill singing. Every few minutes when the music droned to a slower, lower pitch, someone had to jump up and wind the handle very quickly for the record to return to its correct speed of seventy-eight revolutions per minute.

What was your favourite music on 45 rpm and 33 rpm long play records?

When I was about ten, Mum and Dad bought a record player to share between us. It was electric and played three speeds with differing size records. It also had a spindle for six records at a time. Soon after, stereophonic sound was invented which we thought gave a breathtaking clarity to any music.

With five children, we all had our different likes and dislikes. My older brothers enjoyed pop music, David loved classical and opera, and Margaret and I preferred folk and jazz. The gramophone became the most popular item in the house, and we had to draw up a music roster for playing records.

Unlocking more listening and watching memories

Did you ever receive a telegram? Was it good or bad news?

How did you feel when you opened the door to see a telegram boy?

Did you ever have to ring an emergency telephone number? Why?

Did you have a local telephone operator? Did she listen in?

Do you recall the special wartime propaganda programmes?

What was the most memorable event you heard on wireless?

When did you buy your first TV set? How old were you? How big was the screen?

How excited were you when you first saw TV in your own home?

What were your favourite programmes?

When did you buy a colour TV? How old were you?

Did you stop going to the cinema when TV arrived?

Combination TV-radio-record players were available all in one, did you have one?

What happened if you wanted to play a record while Mum and Dad wanted to watch TV?

What has been the most significant technological change you or your parents remember, and how did it affect you?

Can you accept technological change easily? Do you have a computer, digital camera or mobile phone?

How do you adapt to the changes?

Music, theatre and art

School plays, musicals, recorders, Laurel and Hardy.

Did you ever learn to play an instrument? What was it? Did you ever want to learn an instrument but didn't? What instrument would you have chosen?

My parents were not very musical and Dad's ability to pitch and follow tunes was not one of his greatest attributes. He used to sing a song called, *Little Billy Williams*, about a little lad who found some cigarettes, got dizzy and fell onto the tramway lines. We had difficulty following the tune until, one day we heard a musical hall artist sing it properly. From then on, we all joined in with great gusto whenever Dad sang it, sometimes too enthusiastically. Dad suspected we were being cheeky, and he was right.

My three brothers and sister all had lessons to learn the piano. Not one of them kept up their disciplined practise so, when it came to my turn, Mum didn't want to waste more money, and I never got the opportunity to learn. I took up guitar during the skiffle era and have played it ever since. My brother, Philip, learned trombone for a while in his school band, and I think my sister, Margaret, played the triangle and recorder.

Did you ever join a group to play or sing? Did you perform as a solo artist? What sort of music did you perform?

Being a Methodist I couldn't help but embrace resounding music and stirring hymns. My singing voice became very strong from regular chapel attendance and when I left school in 1955, music was a big part in my life. I joined a folk and jazz club and, with my school friends, Michael and Tet Powell, started a skiffle group. They played guitar much better than I did, so I concentrated on washboard. It was quite sophisticated, with a sandpaper block and cymbal that added colour to the percussion.

There were six members of the group with two guitars, a banjo, tea chest base, washboard and Okophone (its name derives from "Okni", a phonetic for "Hockney"). The Okophone was created from the zinc sound box of an old upright, wind-up gramophone. A smaller sound box was called the Oknibone. A kazoo placed in the small end piece created a trombone sound.

Where did you perform? How many in the group? How long did it last? How did the audience react?

I began singing with a jazz band, then became a compere at the Bradford Students Club. The club attracted the best names in jazz in the country, including Acker Bilk and Humphrey Lyttleton. On Saturdays, the jazz sessions lasted all night, much to the annoyance of my mother and father who thought evil was to become me. They didn't understand the music was my adrenalin—no drugs—I just wanted to listen and dance to the music until early morning.

My parents' interests lay in museums and art galleries, or passive outdoor attractions. Weekends or holidays with them meant we may be observing bees making honey or studying a fine collection of Roman spears and arrowheads. The Bradford Art Gallery held an interesting collection of period oil paintings and old traction steam engines, and with each change of an exhibition, a new family visit was organised.

We visited the lovely old abbeys or cathedrals, and our favourite was Bolton Priory where my mother and father began courting. After my father died, David made a beautiful and sensitive photo collage of my mother seated on an ancient gravestone, with the abbey in the background. Some of my mother's ashes have now been scattered at Bolton Abbey.

When was the first time you went to a theatre or art gallery? Do you recall what you saw or what impressed you?

An advantage of growing up in an industrial mill town, was that many of the rich mill owners became philanthropists, generously supporting the arts and theatre—something gratefully acknowledged by the local citizens.

Dad loved music halls and live theatre, and often took David and me to the balcony of the Alhambra Theatre. Latecomers who stood at the back got in for only sixpence, with half price for children. We saw Laurel and Hardy in a live performance there. They seemed different in real life. Hardy was fatter, and had a bright red face that wasn't obvious on black and white film.

Did you have a passion for drawing or painting? Do you still paint or draw? Has any of your family inherited your talent?

Paul, my eldest brother did many sketches in his teenage years, and I remember a school project for which he made a wonderful model of a village, with drawing pins and flour paste painted green on top to represent trees. I thought it was the cleverest thing I had seen.

My brother David went on to become one of the world's great artists.

Did you ever act in a play? What part did you portray? Were you a member of an amateur dramatic group? Did you act, produce, direct or help out? Did you get first night nerves?

My brothers, sister and I joined in amateur theatre at the local Sunday school. Norman and Norah Todd were Sunday school teachers who had a fantastic talent for creating children's theatre. They wrote the scripts and songs, with the words fitted to popular classical music. I affectionately remember the discipline of rehearsals, learning lines and the adrenalin pumping performances on first nights.

Unlocking more music, theatre and memories

Were you given an opportunity later in life to learn a musical instrument?

Did you take the challenge? Can you read music?

What was your favourite piece of music? Who played or sang it?

Have you ever been moved by music or art? Can you describe your feelings?

Did it change the way you looked at art or listened to music? How?

Has a film or play ever left a lasting impact on you? Which one, and why?

Were you interested in ballet, dancing or singing?

Did you ever write short stories or poetry? Have you kept them?
Include them in your story!

Music halls were popular entertainment, did you go to a music hall theatre?

Which artists performed at that time?

Did you ever go to live theatre, pantomime, or plays?

Did you find theatre exciting? What did you see?

Did you ever go to cinema matinees? How much did it cost?

Who was your favourite film star? What film?

Wurlitzer theatre organs were installed in larger cinemas;
did you ever have a singsong?

What were your favourite sweets to buy at interval time?
Did you ever roll them down the aisle?

Did you go to a drive-in cinema? Did you get up to mischief with your
girlfriend/boyfriend in the back seat?

New homes, new lands

Cruise ships and boat people,
"re-education camps" and hostels.

We all smile in the same language.

AUTHOR UNKNOWN

FROM LEBANON

Which year did you leave your homeland? Who met you when you arrived there?

Souad Daizli (nee Chaaban) will never forget June 5, 1967. It was the day she stood on Australian soil for the first time to embrace a new country, a new culture and a new family. She will also not forget because it was the first day of the Six Day War, between Israel and her homeland, Lebanon.

The concern that the new war might involve family and loved ones in Lebanon dampened the warm welcome Souad received from her new husband, Ramzi, and his relatives in Sydney.

Did you enter into an arranged marriage? What were your feelings at the time? What was your wedding day like? Did you enjoy a honeymoon? Where?

She was sixteen-and-a-half, alone and apprehensive. Her engagement and marriage by proxy had been arranged by her family in Lebanon. Although there were already some family connections with his family (Souad's older sister had married Ramzi's brother) Souad had never met her husband. All she had seen was a photograph of her betrothed.

How did you feel leaving your homeland and family? Were you sad or excited? Did your new homeland make you feel welcome?

Souad insists everyone was very kind, and her Australian neighbours were warm and hospitable, but it was nearly two years before she began to accept her new life there. She understood her homesickness and sadness were problems she alone could resolve. Even religious contact was limited—there were only forty Muslim families in Sydney. It was very different to today.

Have you ever returned
to your homeland?

In 1982, Souad, Ramzi and their children returned to Lebanon. They wanted to see relatives and have their children experience their parent's homeland. Nineteen months later, they decided to come back to Australia. The children had found it difficult to fit into school life in Lebanon and, as the civil war escalated, safety also became a concern.

"Australia has been good to us", says Souad. They felt welcomed, they felt Australia was their home— and their children's, children's home.

Rowayda, their eldest daughter is now a loans manager with the ANZ bank; Rashid, their first-born son, is an electrical engineer; and Sophia is a manager at Payless Shoes. Their youngest son, Ahmad, plans the store layouts for Big W.

Souad and her family continue to enjoy celebrating the festivals of their homeland, as well as embracing and sharing all that Australia has to offer.

FROM VIETNAM

I first met Loc Nguyen in 1980, and even then I was struck by his presence that reflected a gentleness and inner strength. He is slight of build, his hair is greying now and he wears gold wire frame spectacles. He lives with his beautiful Vietnamese wife, Van, and son Lawrence in a comfortable two-storey home in suburban Sydney. They are keen gardeners and grow hundreds of different species of roses. Like their life now, their garden is tranquil and peaceful, very different to the horror and difficulties they faced over twenty-five years ago.

What was life like in
Vietnam?

Loc was interested in people and stories, and Vietnam had plenty of both. He took a degree in journalism and qualified at Van Hanh University, practising for two years before the escalating war induced him to register for army service.

Were you involved in military action in Vietnam? In what capacity? How long were you involved?

After nine months of rigorous training, Loc assumed the rank of Warrant Officer and was eventually promoted to Second Lieutenant, until his internment by the communists in a "re-education" labour camp. The camp was primitive, with poor living conditions. It operated under sufferance of a starvation diet and, to survive, the prisoners tried to source their own vegetables to make simple soups.

When were you released? And why?

It was only because Loc's father had died fighting for Vietnam's independence against the French colonialist that Loc was released after three and a half years. Loc was fortunate. Other prisoners had no idea if they were to remain interned for five, ten or twenty years. The higher the rank of officer, the longer the need to re-educate.

How did you come to Australia? Did you have to leave loved ones behind?

On his release, Loc and his wife, Van, discussed the possibility of leaving Vietnam for a new life in Australia but, to get there, money was needed to pay a boat owner. Negotiations to take them all, and pay later, failed. The boat owner would only agree to take one parent and a child, leaving the remaining family behind as security against repayment of the loan. The boat owner wanted gold or cash. Rates were based on the US dollar, and fluctuating prices meant the repayment could be a great deal more, or less, than the current rate.

Loc and Van spent many restless days and nights talking through their future. How many years would they be separated? Would they ever see each other again? Would they be accepted in the new country? How long would it take to save and repay the loan? Van already had a brother and sister living in Australia, so Loc thought it better that she took Lawrence first, but Van spoke no English and the journey could be dangerous. As a man, he could better protect himself and their son, so it was decided Loc should be the first to leave.

They were deeply in love, and with a son they both cherished. It was the hardest decision they have ever made.

The week before it was time to depart, Loc and Van promised each other that if in time there was no contact, the other should feel free to remarry.

Loc and Lawrence sadly said their goodbyes, and boarded the fishing boat. There were more than two hundred people on board the vessel that measured just eighteen metres by three metres wide.

Was it a difficult journey?

Men were put at the bottom of the boat, to sit or squat on the floor. Women and children were put on the top deck as seasickness affected them more than others. The boat owner and his family and relatives commandeered the open top deck.

Occasionally Loc managed to take two year old Lawrence to the ventilation window for fresh air. The sea was often so rough they feared they would never reach land again. There was little food available, but because of sickness, most people drank only water for five days and six nights until the boat disembarked its human cargo on a US oilrig, just off the coast of Malaysia.

The US contacted the Malaysian authorities to have the boat people sent to Indonesian waters, and placed them on a deserted island until the Indonesian government took them to a refugee camp.

Loc and Lawrence stayed in the camp for over a year until an Australian delegation came to interview the inmates. They were accepted as refugees with legitimate entry into Australia. A boat took the refugees to Singapore where they boarded a Qantas flight to Australia. They arrived in March 1980 and, together with other Vietnamese, were sent to the East Hills hostel, near Liverpool on the outskirts of Sydney.

Remember When...

Could you speak English or be able to make yourself understood? How were you accepted when you first arrived? Where did you live? How much money did you have?

The very first thing Loc asked the welfare officer at East Hills was for help to sponsor his wife, Van, for possible entry into Australia. The only option the officer had at that time was to initiate the necessary documents for sponsorship. Loc was given a receipt number 217 which he forwarded to Van. In Vietnam, Van contacted the Australian authorities and quoted the sponsorship number, and was also told she would have to wait.

The hostel taught the refugees English, and Lawrence started kindergarten.

What sort of work did you get when you first arrived? How difficult was it to save money when you first arrived? Did you have to work long hours, or have two jobs?

Five months later, they moved to Carramar, and lived with the family of a friend Loc had met in the Indonesian refugee camp. His friend had five children of his own, but his wife and two daughters were still in Vietnam, in the same situation as Loc's wife. It was far better for Lawrence to have a family around him, and Carramar was much closer to industry. Loc applied for and got a factory job at URI, the company where I also worked.

With a steady job, Loc was able to send money on a regular basis to support Van and his mother in Vietnam. At the same time, he was repaying the loan from the original boat owner and trying to live frugally on a domestic budget. It left him nothing for special occasions and Lawrence had to go without many things other children could take for granted. Even birthday presents had to be denied him. Lawrence visited URI sometimes with his dad and one day a kindly Russian woman, Lola, took him to Fairfield to buy him a present. His eyes lit up, and the smile on his face reached from ear to ear.

What happened to the family you left behind?

Van wrote to Loc to suggest that, rather than money, he should send her goods that were scarce or unavailable in Vietnam. That way she could sell them for much more than their worth in Australia, and be able to repay the boatman more quickly. So Loc selected special fabrics and sent them to his wife, but sometimes the parcels disappeared, and the whole exercise of saving had to begin again.

Eventually Loc was able to secure a personal loan of $2,000 from a local bank, and this, together with his savings, meant the boat loan could be repaid. At last Van was free to travel, but her visa application had still not been processed. Then, when a friend's wife arrived, whose application number was much later than Van's, Loc realised something was amiss.

He copied the article I had written about him in our company newsletter, *Shoptalk*, and sent it with a letter to Bob Hawke, the Prime Minister of Australia. Soon after, the Australian Embassy in Vietnam requested the Department of the Interior to look for Van so they could process her application.

When contact was made at last, Van was able to show them the receipt for her early application. The authorities had inadvertently placed her application at the bottom of a pile, and when she finally saw it, her photograph had been eaten away by cockroaches and was unrecognisable.

Finally, six years from the time they separated, Van flew into Sydney and was reunited with her husband and a son she could barely recognise.

Was there an opportunity to study? What subjects did you take?
Where did you study?
What was the result?
Has the result helped you get a better job?

Loc believed education was the way to achieve a better standard of living for the family and he studied at night to earn a degree in languages, a Bachelor degree in teaching and a Master of Arts in Applied Linguistics. He is now a teacher.

Young Lawrence also went to university, and is now a pharmacist, with four pharmacies in New South Wales and two in Queensland.

Unlocking more memories of new homes, new lands

Were you born in this country?

When did you, your parents or your ancestors first arrive here?

Could you speak English? Do you remember what English sounded like before you understood it?

How did you cope with language and communication?

What transport brought you? How long did it take?

Did you make new friends on the journey? Are you still friends?

Did you have difficulties or misunderstandings with Immigration or Customs officials?

What difficulties were they? How did you deal with the problems?

How difficult was it to leave family in your homeland?

Did you have any funny experiences adapting to a new culture?

Are you homesick for country, family or friends? Have you ever returned?

Were there any special local customs or traditions in your area? What were they?

How many of your family were left in your homeland?

Did you, or do you write to them? Have you kept the letters?

How do you feel about this country now, compared with when you arrived?

Have you officially become an citizen of this country? At what age, and when?

How did you adapt to life here? Are you happy you settled here? Why?

Where did you live when you first arrived?

How did your children cope with school? Was it difficult to learn and adapt?

What were your feelings? Did you want to stay?

What was the best part of living in your homeland?

Who would you see? Where would you go?

How did older family members cope with the new culture and life here?

New Year

Auld lang syne, dragon dancers, a lump of coal
and a piece of fruit.

How did you celebrate New Year as a child? Were you allowed to stay up? Did you participate in any unusual customs on New Year's Eve? What were they?

In some countries people are very superstitious about New Year. In my home town of Bradford, some people believed if a dark haired person, carrying a piece of fruit in one hand and a piece of coal in the other, was the first visitor after midnight on December 31, the household would have good luck all year round. The coal represented warmth for the house, and the fruit meant sufficient food for the year.

I was happy to indulge in this superstition around our neighbourhood, especially as it meant I received almost a week's wages for just a few home visits. (Personally, I never believed in my own powers.)

In Australia, I shared my first New Year with new friends. At midnight each person took a saucepan or frying pan—anything that was metal or could make a noise—and in a single conga line procession we went into the street banging our instruments and shouting, "Happy New Year". I am not so sure all the neighbours appreciated our festive gesture, but it was great fun.

Were there different New Year celebrations or customs in your family?

The Chinese New Year is based on the lunar calendar so it does not occur until around mid January or February. Before the end of the old year, houses have to be completely cleaned to rid them of all the bad luck accumulated over the past year. In the first three days of the new year the house cannot be swept, or good luck will be swept away.

Chinese friends tell me that knives and scissors are hidden away during this period, because to use a knife during the first three days of celebration also cuts off any good luck the new year brings in.

Fifteen days after Chinese New Year, when the full moon shines, the lantern festival begins. Coloured lanterns, sometimes made by the children, decorate homes and streets. This is also the time when small red envelopes with money are exchanged, and the lion and dragon dancers parade through the streets, winding in and out of houses and businesses to bring good luck.

Unlocking more New Year memories

How did your parents celebrate New Year?

Do you remember the first time you participated in New Year?

How old were you? Where did you live at that time?

Do you recall any special traditions or customs celebrated by your family? What were they?

Have you continued the tradition in your own family?

Did you make lanterns or help decorate the home?

How did you celebrate New Year as a teenager? Where did you go? With whom?

Did you participate in any unusual customs on New Years Eve? What were they?

Some cities have large outside gatherings to count the New Year in – did you ever attend a public party? What did it feel like to be part of a large crowd?

If you lived in a different country/place, does the celebration differ from where you now live? How?

Are there any other customs or traditions you remember or practise today?

No place like home

Scumble paint, the dunnyman and southerly busters.

Where did you live as a child? What was the house like?

The Hockneys first lived in a small terrace close to the city with an outside "tippler" toilet and no bathroom. Personal washing was on a Friday night in a zinc bath in front of the fire.

After that we lived in a four-storey terrace house built of natural Yorkshire stone, though the natural colour had been blackened by belching dark smoke from industrial and domestic coal burning chimneys.

Did the house have a view over the sea or countryside? How many houses have you lived in? How did they differ? What were they made of?

I don't remember too much of our first house, but from the attic bedroom of our Eccleshill house, the view up Airedale was spectacular. Lush green fields flowed to the distant valley villages of Greengates and Apperley Bridge. No matter the weather, this view remains in my heart. In winter, snow transformed the landscape to a white, crisp wonderland. In summer, the sweet fragrance of fresh mown hay filtered up from the small farms down the valley. In spring and autumn, vivid rich colours stirred my soul.

How many rooms did they have? Was it a house or apartment? Was it single storey or double? Was it free-standing or a terrace? Did you have to share a room or bed? With whom? When did you get your own room?

The Eccleshill house provided my parents with their own bedroom. My sister had a small bedroom for herself, while Paul and Philip, David and I shared front and back attic bedrooms. There was a proper bathroom inside the house, and a flushing toilet that was frequently visited in the early days, more from novelty than necessity.

The house was a "through terrace" meaning it had a front and back door. There was a living room, kitchen, and a front room with a moquette three-piece suite used only for special occasions. A large stone cellar with a bay window kept food and drinks cool in summer. It was a long time before we ever had the luxury of refrigeration.

A back lane separated the garden access from the house. Mum grew vegetables and flowers, and there was a miniscule block of lawn, and when a horse and cart passed by, we chased it with a shovel to pick up the horse manure and put it on our rhubarb!

There were two outhouses with middens (large slab stone roofs) one for coal storage, the other for bicycles and garden tools.

Both front and back entrances to the house had a vestibule, though the front was rarely used except for special visitors and strangers. The kitchen had an extendable leaf dining table and chairs, a gas cooker and a sink within a cupboard. The floor covering was linoleum with a rag rug in front of the fireplace. A cupboard, sideboard and two easy chairs in front of the fire made the room look smaller than it actually was.

On the side of the cupboard, a slim piece of paper had been stuck there as a measuring guide. Our names were marked on the paper and, each year, on our birthdays, we were measured against the cupboard to see how much we had grown. For accuracy, shoes were discarded and we stood with heels flush to the base of the cupboard, shoulders back and head upright. Mum or Dad slid a steel rule over the head to touch the cupboard, and the measurement was marked off with pencil. I was thrilled when I had grown an inch or two.

Rooms were simply decorated. Wallpaper was scarce and expensive during the War years, and Dad painted the walls and ceiling with distemper (a powder and water mix solution). There was only a limited range of colours, so Dad mixed them to create his own shades. Then, with a sponge dabbed in a darker colour, he created patterns on the walls. On the front and back doors, he used a scumble paint which, when applied correctly, gave an impression of timber. Dad being very artistic, created a wonderful picture of the sun and its rays, very different from any of our neighbours, and it looked very warm and welcoming.

Have you ever returned to see your childhood house? Was there an emotional attachment?

I went back to the Hutton Terrace house in Bradford in 2002, and the owners invited me up to the attic to have a look at the view. Housing now blots the landscape I loved, and the house appeared very tiny to how I had remembered it.

When I came to Australia I was surprised to see suburban houses on individual blocks of land. I had assumed that most houses would be terraces, but then I had a lot to learn about Australia.

The first house we rented was an L-shaped, one bedroom fibro home. It had an outside dunny, which the "sanitologist" emptied every week during the wee small hours. It backed on to the Koala Park at West Pennant Hills and wombats wandered into the garden and garage. It scared the life out of me when I first saw one, but we eventually became quite attached to each other. The garden had fruit bearing plum and apple trees, and a lawn that seemed to grow overnight. The house was hot in summer and cold in winter. On hot summer evenings, neighbours told us to open the front and back doors to let in the nightly southerly buster to cool the house. It made all the difference to a good night's rest.

Unlocking more "no place like home" memories

What power services were available: water, gas, electricity, generator or pumps?

How was the home heated or cooled?

Was the cooking stove wood fired, gas or electric?

Were there any peculiarities about the house?

Was it haunted?

Did you have hawkers come to the house?

Did the milkman, iceman, teaman, icecream van, rag and bone man, gypsies, coal, "dunnyman" or "sanitologist" call?

Describe the labour saving devices used in the home?

If you ever revisited your home later in life, did it look much smaller?

How had the neighbourhood changed? Is it more up-market or down-market than when you lived there? More built-up or modernised?

Were some of the same neighbours still there?

Did it seem time had stood still and you had moved forward?

Was there much you could still recognise—the tree where you built your cubby house; the hill where you raced your billycart; the local park where the birds swooped on your head in nesting time?

Politics and unions

Bias, singing and women's work.

Were you politically active? Did you discuss politics at home or was it a taboo subject?

My father was extremely political, and taught us how to assess the bias of media journalism. Dad always wanted to discover truth, or as close as he could. Newspapers and magazines covering the right and left of the political spectrum dropped through our letterbox on a daily basis. He then read the main topic headlines and showed us how much reporting varied with each publication. I soon learnt to evaluate the politics of a story and to question the "statements of facts" presented in newspapers before I reached a final decision on topics.

Voting was not compulsory in the UK so party candidates worked hard to express their policies. Public meetings were part of the electoral campaigns and there seemed to be much more personal contact with politicians than today. My mother and father voted for different parties and Mum used to sing a song around the house, "Vote, vote, vote for Mr. Taylor, he is way the better man."

Were you a member of a union? Which one? How active were you?

When I arrived in Australia in 1964, women were still on half wages for virtually the same job. I always thought it very unjust. I had been a member of the Shopworkers union in England and became a member of the Shop and Allied distributive workers union in Australia. Unions seemed much more powerful in Australia than England even though most delegates were Scots or from the north of England.

Unlocking more political and union memories

How old were you when you first voted?

How did you feel being able to vote for the first time?

Did your spouse or parent try to influence your voting?

How did you decide your voting intent: newspaper, meetings, radio, friends, brochures?

Did your mother and father openly support a political party?

Which one was it? Were they members? Have you joined a political party?

Has a known political policy improved your life?

Do you perceive a difference in politicians today compared to the time you began to vote?

Were you a member of a union? Which one? How active were you?

Do you believe unions improved working conditions in the past? How?

How do unions differ today from yesteryear?

Women were often paid half men's wages. When did you/they start receiving a comparable salary?

Did you come from a totalitarian state? What were living conditions like in such a country?

Were you ever a member of a political party? If so, why did you join?

Do you remember going to any political rallies in your youth?

What were you passionate about to change the world?

Was there an outstanding speaker, and did he change the way you thought?

Did you ever participate in protest marches? Were they peaceful?
Were you ever arrested as a protester? What do you remember most about the causes you marched for?

Remembrance days and commemorations

ANZAC Day, poppies and two-up.

Did you ever march or attend a remembrance service?

To be there in a crowd, watching old soldiers pass by is an unforgettable experience. There is a sort of reverence that seems to communicate itself between marchers and observers.

I had sometimes watched a small gathering of the British Legion in England, and wore a poppy in remembrance of those who had fallen. ANZAC Day in Australia seems somehow different. There is a unique spirit that captures the crowds as old soldiers march alongside young people who walk in place of their remembered fathers, brothers or grandfathers, and whose medals they proudly wear. Perhaps it is the camaraderie of ordinary or extra-ordinary men and women? Perhaps it is the size of the march that overwhelms us?

The solemnity of this day is sacred, but from it bursts a mixture of tears, laughter and fun as games of two-up, a middy or two of beer, and wartime recollections flow to the end of the day.

Unlocking more remembrance day memories

Were you or a member of your family in active service?

Where were you stationed?

What was your/your parent's/grandparent's true age when they
signed up to go to war?

Were any family members or friends killed in action?

How were you informed? What was your reaction at the time?

What were your innermost feelings when you pulled a trigger aimed at killing a person?

Were any family members or friends wounded?

Where were they, and how were they treated?

How did you react emotionally to their being wounded?

Were you or a member of your family or friend captured and held as a POW?

In which country were you/they captured? How were you/they treated?

How did you react emotionally to capture?

Were letters written to each other?

Do the letters still exist? What is written in them?

Did you ever have the opportunity of helping a comrade? What did you do?

What were your feelings about war when you returned?

How did you adapt to civvy life again?

Were you or members of your family in civil defence or land army?

Did you make friends? Where did you work on the land or near home?

Have you or any member of your family marched in remembrance ceremonies?

What does the day mean to you?

How did you feel watching or marching with old comrades?

There are many stories to share with comrades. Which is the most vivid you
remember or have been told?

Schooldays

Learning to read, avoiding sport and report cards.

Do you remember your first day at school? Were you anxious, excited or scared?

I first went to primary school at four years of age but before that I had followed my brother to his school each day. There was a teacher, Mrs. Bates, who took an interest in me and lent me a *Ring of Roses* book to learn the words at home. By the time I went to school, I had read all six stories and felt quite proud that I knew the stories when others were just beginning to learn.

Did you have good teachers? How did they affect your learning?

I never really liked school, but I think it was because the War claimed young teachers for service and we were left with the older teachers who probably preferred to have been retired. Their style of teaching was through fear and punishment, an attitude not conducive to learning. The only time I loved a subject was when the teacher was passionate about it and shared their enthusiasm with us.

What were other schools like? What lessons did you like?

For Souad Daizli, school in Lebanon was very different. In primary school, lessons were taught in Arabic, but in high school they were taught in French. Souad had loved the challenge of maths, but found the high school lessons in French much more difficult to understand.

Other than education, schools provided little else. Textbooks, exercise books, and stationery all had to be supplied by parents. Uniforms were compulsory, with no exceptions permitted.

Souad recalls that she made every possible excuse to avoid playing sports. Many years later, when she saw her own children join in school sports in Australia, and saw their fun, she wished her own excuses in Lebanon had not been so effective.

Unlocking more schoolday memories

How did you feel meeting other children?

Did you have friends starting school with you?

What was the name of your first school? Where was your last school?

What did your school look like from outside or inside classrooms?

When you first started school what did you write on?

How did you get there: on foot, bus, bicycle, horse?

Did you get school reports to take home? Did parents have to sign them?

Did you write with nibbed pens and who filled the inkwells on your desk? Did you get stars, in your book for good work? How well did you do in exams?

Did you have homework? How many hours did homework take you?

Did you have to wear a uniform? If not, what did you wear?

Did you carry books in a satchel or small suitcase?

Were you ever naughty? What did you do? What punishment did you get?

What playground games did you play? With whom?

Did you wag school? How did you get away with it?

Was there a teacher who made a difference to your life? How?

What were your favourite subjects? Why? What were the subject choices like?

Did you like school? Do you wish you had worked harder or paid more attention?

What was the most useful thing you learnt at school?

Were you a school or house captain or prefect? Did you enjoy the role?

Do you still have contact with school friends?

What age did you finish school? Why?

Did you go on to university/college or participate in work training?

What subjects did you take? Did you gain a degree?

How did your degree or education make a difference to your life?

Shopping

Milk in bottles and bread in horsecarts.

Do you recall the older style stores with large counters? Did you shop there often? What items did you usually buy?

I very rarely went into large department stores, except Woolworths, Marks and Spencer or British Home Stores, mainly because others were "posh", and more expensive. Besides, many stores had uniformed commissionaires on the door and they'd tell kids like me to "Op it!"

Goods were displayed inside glass partitioned counters. There was no self-service and a salesgirl or salesman stood behind each counter waiting to serve you.

How did you pay for goods and receive your change?

In larger stores, your payment and sales docket were placed in a cylinder, then whizzed overhead along wires to a central, elevated cashier's office. I loved watching the cylinders fly to and fro, and to guess which one was returning with our change.

How did you shop for groceries, vegetables and meat? Did you have to queue at each store? How long did it take to shop? Did you shop everyday? Were milk, bread, tea, ice or soft drinks delivered to your door?

General household shopping differed greatly from the supermarket self-selection of today. Milk, tea, bread, soft drinks and household brushes were brought to your door on a daily or weekly basis. Few people had the luxury of refrigeration, and shopping for fresh food was a daily chore. I was often sent shopping for my mother with a list for the grocer, the butcher and greengrocer. There was always a queue in each store so it took a long time to shop, but the queues were how the local gossip was received.

Did you visit weekly markets? Did you go to browse, listen or buy?

Saturday morning at the market was pure entertainment for me with the market stall-holders' showmanship and persuasive patter. One market trader, called Johnny, always drew a large crowd. He wore a top hat with pound notes stuck around the brim. I saw him offer rainbow coloured umbrellas, emphatic that, as soon as it rained, the colours would wash out. Everybody laughed and bought their bargain umbrella. Johnny had told the truth, the colour did wash out in the rain!

Did you ever eat out at a cafe or restaurant? When was the first time you visited a cafe? Did you feel important?

In Bradford, there was a cafe called Collinsons, which specialised in freshly ground coffee. The aroma of their freshly ground coffee wafted through the streets, enticing shoppers to have a coffee and cake in the cafe. A trio of elderly men played violins and viola on a stage decorated with large potted palms. I thought it very elegant.

Unlocking more shopping memories

Was there a shop or store you really liked to visit? What did it sell?

People often window-shopped when the store was closed. Did you window shop?

Which department stores did you visit?

Which stores from your childhood are still operating? Which stores do you remember that no longer exist?

Did you ever shoplift as a dare? What happened? Do you regret it now?

Did you ever have to buy "unmentionables"? Were you embarrassed?

How did you ask for them?

Sport and recreation

Swan dives.

What was your favourite sport or recreation? At which sport did you excel?

Football, cricket or athletics never aroused great enthusiasm in me, though I loved swimming and was quite proficient.

Soon after starting grammar school, I was invited to be the Blue House captain. I rushed home in excitement, and to relate the news of the forthcoming interschool swimming gala to my parents. I desperately needed some new swimming trunks to replace the hand-me-downs I had used for years. I asked Mum if she could buy me a new pair. With a saddened face, she told me we couldn't afford new trunks but that she would make me a new pair. There was no need for a try on, as they were made to the pattern of the old ones.

On the big day, my new swimmers were wrapped in a towel at the end of the table, and I grabbed the bundle as I headed out of the door to the swimming baths. I excitedly undressed to put on my new trunks but when I opened my towel, my face fell to the floor. There, resplendent, was a hand knitted pair of swimming trunks in battleship grey wool. I hated my mother for this.

I put them on and pulled the thin top elastic as tight as I could to ensure a firm fit around my waist. I knew I would have to wear them, they were the only trunks I had. Some of the lads started scoffing, and asked if I was wearing a tea cosy? These remarks did not help my attitude to the problem.

Then the sports master told me that the lad who was our champion diver was sick, so I was to take his place. I was a useless diver, but regardless of my protests I stood at the end of the diving board thinking only of keeping my arms above my head. All eyes were on me. You could have heard a pin splash as I braced and headed upward for my dive.

I could hear the roar of the crowd from six feet under the water as my body went down... but the trunks stayed on top of the water.

I hurriedly retrieved the trunks under water and pulled them on. When I surfaced, the crowd went mad with the sound of resounding cheers mixed with loud laughter. Terribly embarrassed, I swam to the two chrome bars at the corner of the pool to pull myself out of the water.

Up I went up out of the water... the trunks stayed down in the water.

The place was in pandemonium. Spectators had tears streaming down their faces, some were holding their stomachs with laughter at my entertaining predicament. Somehow, I pulled up the trunks and ran to the dressing room.

Mr Dawson the sports master couldn't speak, but I did.

"No more swimming tonight. Not ever", I said.

Some minutes later, when the laughter and sniggers had subsided, Mr Dawson had convinced me to borrow another lad's trunks to compete in my favourite event. Spurred by my humiliation, I won the breaststroke.

I didn't speak to my mother for a month. But eventually time heals, and I realise she made them not just of necessity, but also of love. However, public sports activities ceased for me after that.

Unlocking more sport and recreation memories

Did you win any certificates or trophies?

Have you pursued sport as a profession or on-going pastime?

Were your parents enthusiastic sports supporters?

Which games and teams did you support as a child, as a young person, as an adult?

What is or was the value of sport to you?

Were your friends participating in the same sports or recreation?

Did you compete together? Who was best? Who won?

What was the highest level of competition you achieved?

Who was your favourite sports person?

What sport did they play?

What make-do equipment did you use for sport as a child?

How well did you play sports when the correct equipment was unavailable?

Did you prefer team sports or individual effort?

Did you have coaching?

Were you a natural at sports?

Other than sport in which recreational activities did you participate:
craft or home hobbies?

What objects did you make?

Sweethearts, courting and getting wed

First kiss, broken hearted, down on one knee and untying the knot.

Who was your first love? Where did you meet? How old were you? What attracted you to your first love?

I was sixteen when I met my first sweetheart. My heart thumped, and I felt I could walk on water. When true love really happened, that first kiss sent flutters to the tips of my toes, I felt exhilaratingly happy. There was another person in this world besides my parents and family who loved me! The experience was new and unabashed.

Were you knowledgeable about sex as a teenager? How were you informed?

My parents had never shared any knowledge of sex or sexuality. Other than "wait until you get married", it was never discussed. Any knowledge I gleaned was from toilet walls and schoolboy chatter. I was very naïve.

How did you cope with your first rejection? How long before you went out with someone else?

My first sweetheart was blonde, blue-eyed, soft and gentle. Hand in hand, we floated down the street, oblivious to passers-by who must have seen clearly that we were in love.

Then, one day came the terrible confrontation when I was told, "It's over". I was plunged into the depths of despair. I felt rejected and scorned. I had shared all my innermost secrets with this person. Was I going to be laughed at for sharing my secrets? How could she have done this to me? I was angry. I felt my life would never be the same again.

Did you have many sweethearts?

Fortunately my teenage male hormones and adrenalin had not died in the process, and other sweethearts gradually embraced my love. The sweetheart cycle happened many times before Miss Right came along.

I had a calmer and more mature feeling when I did meet Miss Right and my happiness moved up another rung of the romantic ladder when I fell in love with her. The day I whispered sweet nothings and promised myself to her, she responded with a shyly whispered, "Yes," followed by a long lingering kiss to seal our love for each other.

Was the hand in marriage asked of the girl's parents? How was it asked? Did both lots of parents approve?

We didn't intend to elope so I had to ask her parents for their permission to marry. I remember feeling very anxious about what their reaction would be.

Will they like me? Will they say no? What would I do then? What happens if they don't consider my future prospects good enough for their daughter?

The anxiety began to test my confidence, so I focussed my thoughts on my marriage to their daughter, not on them.

From your engagement day, how many months or years was it until you married? Why?

When the engagement became official, time was dominated by wedding arrangements: guest lists, honeymoon, where we would live, what furniture to buy. For the first time in our lives we had to make joint decisions and personal choice concessions. Life was suddenly a big learning curve. It was the time independence was lost while personal individuality remained.

Was your marriage a religious or civil ceremony? Where did you get married?

I had friends at that time, who were not at all well off, and got married at the Registry Office because the church ceremony was too expensive. They even had to live with her parents until they could afford their own place. It was a struggle for them in their early years of marriage, but they are still very happy, have four children and live comfortably in a semi-detached house in Yorkshire.

Describe the day you both met at your marriage venue to be married?

When I saw my bride walking towards the altar, I got a lump in my throat. She looked like an angel. Our eyes met, slightly glazed, but I was able to hold back my tears of joy. As we walked down the aisle together as Mr and Mrs Hockney, I felt enormous pride, surpassed only by the realisation that my dream had come true.

Did you remain happy? Did the marriage last? What happened?

The marriage lasted nearly fifteen years. It was not a nasty divorce, in fact it was very civilised. By then the hurt, separation and bad feelings had dissipated. There were no children, so perhaps that is why it was much easier to deal with any problems.

It still took a drastic toll on my emotions. I found it difficult to confide or trust again. I had totally believed in my wedding vows, "for richer, for poorer, til death us do part" and didn't think I'd ever be able to make that promise to anyone again.

How long was it before you met someone else? Was it a successful relationship?

The night I met Helen was at the home of my friends, Bill and Greta Marzouk. Bill was a work associate who had a wonderfully mad sense of humour, and held terrifically outrageous parties. He and Greta had planned a blind date without informing either Helen or me. Bill and Greta's plan worked. I fell head over heels in love that night and have never stopped since, and that was twenty-five years ago!

Perhaps it was because it was the second time around for both of us, but the love, friendship and compatibility has grown stronger each year.

Did your wedding and vows differ from the first time?

We were married at my brother's beautiful home at Dural overlooking the lake. A celebrant conducted the ceremony so we could choose the words that we both thought were appropriate to the promises we made to each other.

Have you any local marriage customs from your province or area you can share in a story?

My Greek friends, Bill and Penny Petinos, were married in a traditional service, with the exchange of laurel wreaths over the heads of the bride and groom. I had never witnessed this custom before and found it

How does the custom
vary from traditional
weddings?

a very beautiful experience. There is a solemnity throughout the service that bursts into joyful frivolity at the wedding reception and culminates with energetic Greek dancing. Participation is expected, and even if the dance steps cannot be followed you are carried along with the throng. It is a total delight, and a sense of togetherness that may be unique to Greek communities.

At the wedding reception, I observed a custom of pinning money on the bride's dress in exchange for a dance with the bride. The more money you pinned on, the longer you could dance. To everyone's amusement, one guest was so caught up in the wedding joy he wanted to pin his Gold Amex card to the bride's dress. I found it all enchanting, but could only afford a dollar note for a couple of steps.

I discovered the practice was adapted from their Cypriot connections. To Bill's knowledge, although money is often presented, it is usually done more discreetly in sealed envelopes.

Unlocking more memories of sweethearts, courting and getting wed

Did you raise your hat for a lady, open a door or walk on the road side of a pavement?

Were you chaperoned?

Where was the most romantic place you were ever taken?

What were the most romantic words ever spoken to you?

Did you or your sweetheart write letters or poetry to each other? What did you write?

Have you kept the letters or poems?

Where did you enjoy your courting? Was it a secret place?

Did you walk your partner home after a night out? How did you get home yourself?

Was there a time you were involuntarily separated by war, jobs or health?

Did you have a bottom drawer or glory box? What items had you collected?
What plans did you make together for the big day?

Did you ever go on holiday with a sweetheart or their family?

Who were your bridesmaids and best man? Did your wedding day satisfy
all your expectations?

Where did you go on honeymoon? Describe what your going away clothes were like?

Have you or your parents been divorced?

How did you/they cope with the separation and finality?

How did you cope when you had your first child?

Some parents and grandparents were eager to advise, but did it make
the parenting task any easier?

How did you feel when you first held your precious bundle?

Did you check everything was in place?

Did you have more children? How many?

What are their names and birth dates? Which city were they born?

Travel

Forty-eight hours in a three-piece suit, wide open spaces and Bali bliss.

When was your first flight in a commercial aircraft? Were you travelling within the country or overseas? Where were you going? Why?

I love travel. Given the opportunity I would always be on my way somewhere. Before I flew to Australia in 1964, I had never been on an aircraft, and felt one should look important when travelling. I wore my three-piece suit especially for the occasion and, with a raincoat over my arm, arrived at Heathrow airport.

After sad farewells, hugs and kisses, I boarded the BOAC 707. I was excited but apprehensive. Had I made the right decision to leave? The aircraft positioned itself at the end of the runway and the take off thrust me firmly back into my seat as we left the ground. The sensation was awesome—I tried to look like a seasoned traveller.

Have you experienced a long haul flight? When was your first experience?

Refuelling stops were not long, though we did have an opportunity to stretch our legs in airports at Rome, Cairo, Delhi, Calcutta, Rangoon, Hong Kong and Manilla before our final stop at Kingsford Smith Airport. The longest leg had been the last six hours from Manila to Australia and I disembarked in a hazy wobble. The trip was considerably faster than the four weeks it took by boat, but it had been forty-eight hours before I could get my three-piece suit off and have a bath.

My suit was virtually attached to my body, and it was hard to keep my eyes open as I was whisked away by my brother and his family to a barbecue with friends. I don't recall being overly friendly that day but it certainly was an early introduction to Ozzie hospitality. I had never seen so much meat!

Remember When...

Have you ever been on a cruise or passenger ship? Was the departure sad or exciting, or both?

The excitement of arriving or departing from Sydney Passenger Terminal is perhaps unique in the world. Where else can you sail right into the city itself? It is an experience shared by migrants and visitors alike and, for many, their first glimpse of Australia is the beauty of a sunrise, a sparkling blue harbour and foreshores scattered with bushland, majestic homes, and the Sydney Opera House.

Have you ever visited the Australian outback? How did the experience affect you?

I went bush for the first time six months after my arrival. I could not comprehend the open space and stopped the car on the road to Hay from Rankins Springs just to look at it. The distant horizon shimmered in the afternoon sun and trees were suspended above the earth in a heat-induced mirage. In every direction there was nothing. The only sound was the purr of the car engine. This was a truly unique experience for me.

Have you wandered off to discover some new place on your own? What or whom did you find?

I have travelled in Asia quite extensively and love the smells, sights and sounds of a seemingly endless throb of life.

I was once in Bali with friends, and I particularly wanted to have time walking on my own. Early one morning, I left the hotel and started walking up the beach. I had left the tourist complex way behind when, about an hour later, I came across a group of adults and children throwing nets into the sea and dragging them back to shore. Some of the children were crouching to remove something from the net. As I approached they looked up and smiled, so I went to see what they were doing. They were pulling tiny wriggling fish from the net and putting them into a round enamel bowl. It seemed that they would need an awful lot to make a sandwich. As communication was restricted to smiles and pointing at the net and bowl, I had no real understanding of what their ultimate task was.

When I returned to the hotel, I asked the room attendant if he knew what they had been doing. He told me that if I had walked into the sand dunes I would have seen a small cane and thatched house and a large pond. The family was too poor to afford a boat and could only catch small fish from the shore. The fish were then emptied from the enamel bowl into the pond where, over time they'd grow until they were big enough to eat.

Despite their poverty, I wondered—who lives the more idyllic life?

Did you pursue your special interests on holidays?

One year, my wife and I decided to go to Thailand for a holiday. We had been before, but this time we were visiting the north and the Golden Triangle. I made enquiries whether there were any Thai storytellers who would like to swap stories and a response came from Atchara Pradit, a child literacy lecturer, at the Srinakharinwot University in Bangkok.

We had never met but somehow greeted each other with the warmth old friends enjoy. Atchara spoke perfect English and we were soon discussing how the University felt storytelling was an important part of their curriculum when a group of visitors from Cambodia interrupted our discussions. They had called in hoping to see Atchara on child literacy ideas because, under the Pol Pot regime, all books in their libraries and schools had been destroyed.

How did you overcome any language differences?

The leader of the five young women was French, the other members of the party were Khmer, and I spoke in English, with the French woman translating into Khmer. I learnt the group was desperately trying to source stories in the Khmer culture and language. I suggested that in their search for stories, a link might be created through children to their grandparents—an idea they greeted with enthusiasm. We shared some experiences together and when I saw their faces, sparkling eyes and smiles as I shared my stories, it brought home to me that no matter what the language, stories can help break the barriers we too often raise.

I keep in touch with Atchara, and have since stayed with her delightful family in Bangkok.

Unlocking more travel memories

Have you travelled to a major city from the country, or vice-versa?

Where did you travel to? What transport did you use?

What were your feelings on leaving family and friends?

What were your feelings arriving in a large city, or small country town?

How did you find accommodation? Where did you live?

In the city or town where you settled, did you have friends or family?

If you have been overseas, where did you visit? Why?

How did you travel?

Did the country meet your expectations? How?

Did you travel alone, with family or friends?

Did you meet new people? Who were they?

Have you kept in contact?

How did you cope with different food and drink?

Did you stay in luxury or basic accommodation?

Was there a special souvenir you brought back with you? What was it?

What was the most exciting journey you ever made?

What was the worst experience you ever had whilst travelling?

How did you feel as a minority in another culture?

Was it people or places that made your trip memorable?

War

War will exist until that distant day
when the conscientious objector enjoys
the same reputation and prestige that the warrior does today.
JOHN F KENNEDY

Were you or any of your family engaged in physical conflict?

War can touch many of us without the physical confrontation of being engaged in combat. At the commencement of the Second World War, my father was at an age where registration for military service was not compulsory. He was an ardent pacifist and conscientious objector so he did not volunteer to enlist.

I was born a month after War was declared, so did not appreciate the circumstances of his decision but, over the years, I have come to realise the courage it took to uphold his conviction. Dad's decision was to affect my mother, sister and older brothers when neighbours verbally and, on occasions, physically abused him.

Were you evacuated or separated from your parents because of war? How long were you apart? Who did you stay with during that time? Were they kind or cruel? Did you get enough to eat?

The British Government had implemented an evacuation policy during the War and thousands of children were sent from major cities to be placed in homes with strangers. I personally know some who did not see their parents again for over five years. There was no time to investigate the suitability of these homes and some children suffered greatly as a consequence.

Remember When…

Did you experience bombing on your city or home? Did you or someone you know lose their home and belongings during a bombing raid?

Were you or any of your family wounded or captured? What happened to them? Did they survive? What were your feelings at that time?

Did you or your family have the opportunity to escape from war and oppression? How did you escape? What memorable experiences can you recall from your war years?

The city of Bradford was bombed on only one occasion, so we did not suffer the horrors of nightly bombing raids that London, Birmingham, Liverpool and Hull suffered. So many did lose their homes and loved ones and I cannot begin to comprehend the terrifying experience, or that of a soldier, sailor or airman returning to find their home a pile of rubble.

I am fortunate, too, in not being able to imagine the heartbreak of the families who stayed home waiting for the return of their fathers, sons or husbands, only to be sent a telegram informing them of their capture or death. There were also those who heard nothing, received no news, and lived with the anxiety of wondering whether their loved ones were alive or dead.

As the War progressed, information on the atrocities of concentration camps began to leak out. We now know of the heroic escapes, often helped by local members of an underground movement, at great risk to their own lives. In mainland Europe families took great risks trying to escape oppression and persecution.

There must be thousands of stories of courage and determination, as well as incredible suffering and hardship. Those who lived through two World Wars and oppression may choose to pass on their stories of those years in the shared hope that we may all learn from those experiences.

Perhaps you are a refugee, or lived in a country that lacked the vision of freedom for you and your family. There are stories to tell. If you prefer, you could share the good things, rather than dwell on painful memories. Consider the circumstances when people helped, perhaps at risk to themselves. Maybe help was just a cup of tea, a kind word, a night's lodging or some food, but was appreciated or needed by you at that time.

Unlocking more war memories

Were you in the army, navy, air force or resistance during a war?

Were you conscripted or did you volunteer? How old were you?

How did you get along with your superior officers?

Were you promoted in rank during war?

Where were you posted? How long were you away?

How did you get food? Was it rationed? What food was available?

What do you most remember from your wartime experience?

What was communication like with your family back home?

Do you find it hard to talk about, even now?

Did your experiences affect your future way of life? How did war change you?

Are there stories of bravery in your family?

Did your family suffer or benefit financially from war?

What do you remember about your homecoming?

How were you able to settle back into civilian life after your experiences?

How did you or your parents/grandparents cope during war years?

How has war affected you personally?

Do you support a peace movement or refugee organization? Why? Why not?

What do you hope your grandchildren will learn from your experiences?

What we wore

Hand-me-downs, shoestring ties,
bobby socks and unmentionables.

What style of clothes did you wear when you were young?

It was another era. My grandma sat in her rocking chair in front of the fire, gently pushing herself back and forth. She always wore grey woollen stockings and black thick-soled shoes with a strap. Her dress was draped with a wool-chequered shawl across her shoulders. When she stepped into the street in cold weather she, like the many elderly ladies of that time, lifted her shawl over the top of her head to keep out the chilly breeze.

Did you have to wear hand-me-downs or second hand clothing? Did you mind or were you ashamed? Did your mother or grandmother make clothes for you? What did they make? Did you like wearing them? Were they or you skilled at making your own clothes? Did you have a sewing machine? What kind was it?

When I was growing up, most of the clothes people wore were practical and had very little to do with fashion or style. Having something sturdy to wear was far more important than how people looked, and hand-me-downs were common in large families.

My mother made most of our clothing. She had a treadle Singer sewing machine that produced shirts, short trousers, jackets and overcoats.

When I first went to grammar school, my parents could not afford a blazer for the school uniform so my mother made one for me. She even embroidered the school badge on the pocket. I thought she was very clever until I arrived at school and saw all the other boys had blazers that had been professionally tailored. Mine was noticeably different.

Did you follow the fashion trends or did you prefer to be an individual? What did you wear?

The fashions of my time were dependant on whether you chose to be a teddy boy, a groupie, or a hippie or beatnik. Teddy boys wore hair plastered with Brylcreem and brushed in a DA style ("ducks arse" style). Their jackets were knee length with narrow drainpipe trousers, fluorescent socks and blue or black crepe soled shoes. Shirts had black piping around the collars and cuffs, complimented by a shoestring tie.

Groupies wore well cut suits, round collared shirts with slimline ties and winklepicker shoes fashioned to a fine pointed toe. Overcoats were discarded for camel coloured duffle coats made from a material called Batley Mungo. It was made from old rags, and was especially warm for those who rode Vespa and Lambretta scooters.

Then there were the hippies or beatniks, pot-smoking peace lovers who became the flower people. Simple clothes, based on Indian or Asian colours and materials, were worn with headbands of flower garlands or wide brimmed hats.

Pop groups such as the Beatles set the trends for hairstyles and clothing. London's Carnaby Street became the mecca for teenage fashion, even though many of the girls in the north still wore near ankle length skirts, bobby socks and sweater tops. Dance crazes also changed fashion, and the jive showed-off the girls' swirling skirts and sometimes their unmentionables.

Jean Shrimpton modelled and introduced the mini skirt worn well above the knee with a wonderful show of leg. The vital statistics of some girls never suited mini skirts, but they were fashionable. Their fat thighs were tight against the small piece of skirt that was stretched to the limit (and sometimes stretched at the seams) just to be trendy.

I never pursued fashion, preferring to dress differently. I wore a bright coloured waistcoat, a yellow bowler hat or a plaid deerstalker, and suede chukka boots that were cheap, comfortable and hardwearing. My mother sewed the waistcoats for me, and I was often asked where I had bought them. I considered it a real compliment for Mum.

The introduction of synthetic materials created a complete new range of fashion possibilities.

Unlocking more memories
of what we wore

Did you wear a school uniform? Was it attractive?

Can you remember the first piece of clothing you purchased
with your own money?

Did you feel conscious about what you wore?

What clothing did you enjoy wearing most?

What clothing did you least enjoy wearing?

What clothes did your parents/grandparents wear? How did they differ
from your fashion?

Did they or you have a "Sunday Best" outfit? What was it?

Were you ever told not to wear something by your parents?

Did you still wear it? What was it?

Was it more important for you to wear fashionable or practical
outfits in your youth?

What were the fashions of your day?

Were your parents horrified by what you wore? Did they influence you?

Did you have to wear a hat to be properly dressed (as well as gloves for the ladies)?

As a woman, did you prefer the new pantyhose to stockings and suspender belt?
Was the difference wearing them very noticeable?

When did you first buy a pair of nylon stockings? How much did they cost?

Did you only wear stockings at weekends?

Did you wear bri-nylon shirts and drip-dry materials in the fifties?

Did the new synthetics make a difference to what you wore? How?

Can you remember the price of fashions? How much of your wage or salary
did you spend on clothes?

How did your attitudes to fashion change as you grew older?

Working life

First job, smoko and back to school.

Did you have a job whilst you were at school? What was it? How much did you get paid?

I delivered newspapers six days a week. It meant being on the job at five every morning come snow, rain or shine. I was quick and reliable so eventually took over four rounds until a school inspector, posing as a recruiter from another newsagent, reported me to the education authorities.

Delivering newspapers meant pushing them through the letterbox on every door. Some letterboxes were narrow and others had a hard spring on the back, which made it difficult to push papers through. It took much longer to deliver door to door that way.

What was your first full time job? What did you do? How much did you earn?

When I left school, I decided to become a display artist (a window dresser in the old terminology) and took a night school course as well as working in shops during the day. It was a forty-eight hour working week, with no extra pay if you had to stay back.

How often did you change jobs? Why? Did you stay in the same job for many years? How many?

I moved to different companies quite frequently, something that was acceptable in the display trade, as the more varied experience you gained the more attractive a proposition you became to an employer.

My career has mainly been associated with design, except when I first came to Australia and worked in a factory. The factory opened my eyes to the work boredom some people endured. Whenever a buzzer announced a tea break, "smoko" or lunch period, everyone downed tools, switched off machines and ran to the canteen. Vincent's or Bex headache powders were shared like cigarettes and taken whether they were needed or not.

I studied for a post graduate diploma in design and,

as soon as possible, took a display job in exhibition design and shop fittings. I was later asked to become a part-time lecturer in postgraduate design studies at University of Technology in Sydney. It was a job I found very fulfilling, and came to an end only because of my worsening deafness when, in fairness to the students, I relinquished the position.

Wherever I've lived, I have performed on stage singing folk songs or acting, and I still remember one school report I received that said,

"When John Hockney learns the classroom is not a stage, only then will he get down to real work".

It's a pity I did not have the confidence then, to disregard those comments.

Unlocking more working life memories

How did you convince your first employer to take you on when you had no experience?

Was a choice of career an easy decision? What was it?

Did you change employment? How often? Why?

Did your parents want you to have a profession or vocation different from the one you chose? Who won? Why?

Was your decision accepted, or was your relationship with them difficult on this issue?

Did you enjoy your working life? How good were your working conditions?

What hours did you have to work?

Were you offered study or further advancement?

Were you promoted within your company, and to which position? What were your responsibilities?

What do you, or did you most enjoy about work? What did you most dislike?

Have you had any or many career changes?

Did you have a mentor who helped or influenced you?

Who did you learn most from in your working life?

Researching your story

A lot of what you write will be written from your memories, but some of you may wish to fill out those memories by consulting old newspapers and magazines available at libraries or old wares shops. They will show costs of goods and details of news and events of the period you are researching.

Your state library will also have information that can be accessed via the web or through your local library computer. Loans from the state library can also be arranged through your local branch for a small fee.

"A picture is worth a thousand words" and family photographs will help bring your words alive. Look especially for old photos showing the fashion of the day, holiday snaps, weddings and photos of family or people you are telling stories about.

School reports as well as birth, marriage and death certificates are absolute gems in verifying dates and names.

There are web sites on naval and commercial shipping records, war records, and census information on family information and general statistics.

Letters can reveal a great deal between family members and friends. My mother retained every letter we sent her, and it is amazing to read them now and look back on where we had been, what we had done and how our opinions have since changed. She also kept all her housekeeping records from the day she married until the day she couldn't write legibly anymore. Local historical societies are usually very pleased to help with local information and can be very useful for details of events, people, and places.

Suggested references for reading and research

Brownstone, David M and Franck, Irene M 1996, *Timelines of the 20th Century*, Little Brown, Boston.

Chronicle of the 20th Century 1999, ed. John Ross, Viking Penguin, Melbourne.

Good Old Days-Good old Ways 1999, ed. Janet Healey, Reader's Digest, Sydney.

Hird, Thora with Barr, Liz 1998, *Book of Bygones*, HarperCollins, London.

Hird, Thora with Barr, Liz 1998, *Book of Home Truths*, HarperCollins, London.

Inserra, Rose 1999, *Celebrations of Festivals in Australia* Vols 1-4, Macmillan Education, Australia.

Miller, Patti 2001, *Writing Your Life*, Allen and Unwin, Sydney.

State Library of NSW catalogue online <http://www.sl.nsw.gov.au/webcat>

Wenborn, Neil 1989, *The 20th Century: A chronicle in pictures*, Hamlyn Publishing Group, Sydney.

Suggested organizations for creative writing or storytelling skills

In Australia

ACT: ACT Storytellers Guild Inc, PO Box 420, Dickson ACT 2602
ACT Writers' Centre, PO Box 23, Griffith ACT 2603

NSW: Australian Storytelling Guild (NSW) Inc, PO Box Q274, QVB Post Office NSW 1230
Website: <http://www.australianstorytelling.org.au>
Blue Mountains Story Circle (NSW) Tel: 02 4784370
NSW Writers' Centre, PO Box 1056, Rozelle NSW 2039

NT: Darwin City Library Darwin NT Tel: 08 89279655

QLD: Queensland Storytelling Guild Inc, PO Box 5895, West End Qld 4101
Queensland Writers' Centre, 535 Wickham Terrace, Spring Hill Qld 4000

SA: South Australian Writers' Centre, PO Box 43, Rundle Mall Adelaide SA 5000
Storytelling Guild of Australia (SA), PO Box 162, Stepney SA 5069

VIC: Storytelling Guild of Australia (Vic) Inc, PO Box 235, Albert Park Vic 3206
Victorian Writers' Centre, PO Box 2936, Fitzroy Vic 3035

WA: Australian Writers' Guild, PO Box 492, Leederville WA 6093
Storytelling Guild Of Australia (WA), PO Box 1170, West Perth WA 6872

In New Zealand
NZ Guild of Storytellers <http://storytelling.org.nz>

In the United Kingdom
The Society for Storytelling <http://www.sfs.org.uk>

The Scottish Storytelling Centre <http://www.scottishstorytellingcentre.co.uk>

In the USA
The National Storytelling Network <http://www.storynet.org>

A note from the author

I am a great fan of the British author Alan Bennett. He ingeniously discovers an extra-ordinariness in ordinary people that he conveys with compassion and humour. Most of his characters are older family members and, to me, his writing is often like looking in a mirror at my own family's life experiences. It is the reason I want to encourage you to rediscover simple memories that you may cherish or hold from your own familiarity with people and experiences.

Some of the most recent rewarding experiences, for me, came from the dementia patients who have responded from within the cocoon of their illness to delight me with their long unspoken memories. My first such experience was with a woman who had not conversed with the staff in her nursing home for over eighteen months. I was giving a storytelling session there, talking about the way clothes were washed in the olden days, and humorously fooling around with a washboard. From the back of the room came a croaky, "That's not how you do it", and she proceeded to show me how to hold the washboard and tell me in no uncertain terms how clothes were washed properly!

The road to this book, and my journey as a professional storyteller, began in July 1996, when I walked into a library and picked up a flyer promoting The Australian Storytelling Guild. I have loved telling stories ever since I was a child, but had not realised there were storytelling organizations. At the first opportunity I attended a meeting of the guild and, from that first visit, I was hooked. A year later, I became an accredited storyteller.

I held the usual perception that stories were only for children, but I gradually realised that adults also enjoy stories—and those in aged care and seniors, perhaps most of all.

Then, about five years ago, three other storytellers and I were asked to entertain a university association dinner. There we were introduced to Robyn Lillianthal, a diversional therapist for Wybena Nursing Home. She asked us to prepare a performance for people in aged care, taking into consideration that some of the audience suffered from dementia. We began working on a programme that included old stories, reminiscences and songs about yesteryear, laced with humour. The performance was called *Days of the Week* and concentrated on the repetitive work involved in organising households. We quickly realised how stories and reminiscing were not only very popular with seniors, but acted as a stimulating programme for hostel and nursing home residents in helping to unlock their precious memories.

We called ourselves The Whimsical Weavers, and its members were Sue Alvarez, Christine Greenough, Judy Eddington and me. My wife, Helen, a nursing sister in aged care, gave the group some well-founded advice and suggestions in those early days. We accumulated old artefacts such as washboards, smoothing irons, carpet beaters, cut throat razors, even a wedding dress—anything that would help trigger distant memories. The combination of stories and songs, created around specific objects and personal situations, boosted the responses to the performance immensely.

I live in the Blue Mountains some one hundred kilometres from Sydney, and much as I loved the companionship of my colleagues and the rewarding enthusiasm for our performances, I decided it was not economically viable, and we agreed to dissolve the group. Sue and Christine renamed themselves The Talespinners and have since developed specific programmes for aged care hostels and nursing homes. At times, I still join them at special festivals and venues.

In 2002, I created a workshop called *Unlocking Memories*, and presented it at the bi-monthly Storytelling Guild meeting. It offered methods for looking at the past, and ways of unlocking memories to create life stories. In 2003 and 2004, the NSW Department for the Ageing invited the Australian Storytelling Guild to present a concert and storytelling workshops designed specifically for Seniors Week. The events were a great success, and I continued to concentrate on developing and refining my workshop ideas, and have also presented them in Singapore, at the Asian Congress of Storytellers. The reaction by participants proved that, regardless of nationality and culture, the idea of unlocking memories is widely accepted and popular.

The reactions to the *Unlocking Memories* workshops in city, country and overseas have been incredibly supportive, and it is due to the response, enthusiasm, and encouragement of those who participated, that this book has been written for young and old alike.

John Hockney, September 2004
email: jhockney@tpg.com.au

First published in 2005

Citrus Press
300/3 Smail Street
Broadway NSW 2007
Australia
© John Hockney 2005
Not to be copied whole or in part without written authorisation

National Library of Australia Cataloguing-in-Publication data:
Hockney, John.
Remember when – how to unlock your life story.
Bibliography.
ISBN 0 9751023 4 6.
1. Hockney, John. 2. Autobiography – Authorship.
3. Autobiographical memory. 4. Authorship. I. Title.

808.06692

Design by Judi Rowe
Printed in Australia by Ligare